Discovering Southern African Rock Art

Southern African Archaeology Series

DISCOVERING SOUTHERN AFRICAN ROCK ART

J. D. Lewis-Williams

David Philip
CAPE TOWN & JOHANNESBURG

First published in southern Africa by David Philip Publishers (Pty) Ltd
208 Werdmuller Centre, Claremont, 7700 South Africa

Second Impression 1996
Third Impression 2000

ISBN 0-86486-167-2

Front cover photo of rock painting by Geoffrey Blundell
(Rock Art Research Unit, Wits University)

DTP conversion by BellSet, Cape Town
Printed and bound by Clyson Printers, 11th Avenue, Maitland 7406

For
JOHN ARGYLE &
DAVID HAMMOND-TOOKE

Contents

Acknowledgements

I am grateful to many people who helped with the preparation of this book. Colleagues and friends kindly commented on drafts; they include, T. A. Dowson, G. Emby, J. and W. D. Hammond-Tooke, A. L. Holliday, T. N. Huffman, E. R. Jenkins, M. O. V. Taylor, L. Wadley, D. and T. Whitley. Lorna Marshall generously permitted publication of six of her photographs, and Megan Biesele has always been willing to share her research and discuss ideas. R. Yates of the Spatial Archaeology Research Unit, University of Cape Town, kindly provided a copy of a western Cape rock painting. The Librarian, Jagger Library, University of Cape Town, allowed me to use photographs and unpublished parts of the Bleek and Lloyd Collection, and Miss L. Twentyman-Jones and Miss E. Eberhard sought out useful material. Mrs Y. Garson and Mrs B. H. Strachan of the Cullen Library, University of the Witwatersrand, provided historical material. The Director and staff of the Local History Museum, Durban, gave access to material in their collection. Claire Ritchie of the Ju/wa Bushman Development Foundation kindly supplied photographs and Mr J. N. F. Binneman (Albany Museum) kindly supplied a colour slide of a painted stone from the Klasies River Mouth excavation from which a black and white copy was made.

The book derives from research conducted by the Rock Art Research Unit, Department of Archaeology, University of the Witwatersrand. The Unit is funded by the Institute for Research Development and the University of the Witwatersrand. The opinions expressed and the conclusions arrived at are not necessarily to be attributed to either institution. D. O. Dowson, C. Jeannerat and M. Ramsay typed the manuscript. I am especially indebted to T. A. Dowson, Research Officer in the Rock Art Research Unit, for interminable discussions about the content of the book, extensive fieldwork and for skilfully preparing the illustrations of San rock art and devising the other diagrams.

1

Ways of discovering rock art

Very few people are fortunate enough to discover an unknown rock shelter filled with ancient paintings. Yet in some of the more remote parts of southern Africa it is still possible to come upon a shallow, rocky overhang that may not have been entered since the last San people (Bushmen) left over a century – perhaps several centuries – ago, and to find rock paintings of breath-taking beauty and intriguing interest. No one who has had this exciting experience will ever forget it.

But there are other ways of discovering San rock paintings that everyone can enjoy. It is with these deeper and more absorbing discoveries that this book is concerned. If the paintings are approached with an understanding of San life and beliefs, this kind of discovery can be made even in shelters that have been known to rock art researchers for decades. Familiar paintings are suddenly transformed and illuminated when they are seen through San eyes; whole new vistas of meaning and subtlety open up.

In addition to the paintings there is another kind of rock art that is found on low, rocky hilltops and rises in the

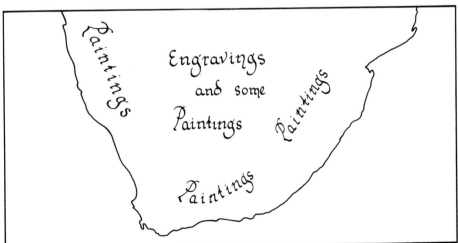

The distribution of rock paintings and engravings in southern Africa.

interior of southern Africa. Thousands of rock engravings have been chipped or cut into rocks scattered in the open. Even though these depictions are often as striking as the paintings, they are, by and large, less detailed and they occur far less frequently in complex groups or 'scenes'. They have therefore attracted less attention from rock art researchers, and much less is known about them. Or, to put it more optimistically, there is even more to be discovered about them.

Both paintings and engravings were encountered by early travellers in southern Africa. Because the artists were still living, the travellers could have asked them what the art meant. In the event, they tended to write about the art but to ignore the artists.

The antagonisms of the colonial situation and the generally low opinion the travellers held of the San stifled all but the most casual interest in any deeper meaning the art may have had. Nevertheless, what they did write is valuable because we can see in their accounts the origin of quite different approaches to southern African rock art.

This book differs from others in that it shows how these approaches developed from those early times. Rock art research grows and expands as researchers discover new ways of seeing 'the facts' and develop new slants on old ideas. Readiness to change one's mind and to advance is the hallmark of a good scientist.

But the changing of one's mind and

A rock engraving site, northern Cape. (Photograph: T. A. Dowson)

View from a rock shelter. T. A. Dowson is tracing paintings.

the direction of one's research in general do not take place in a vacuum. All new scientific theories and explanations develop within the matrix of existing theories and explanations, or rather as a reaction against the inadequacies of older explanations. It cannot be otherwise, for each scientist cannot start from scratch. This is not to say that all new ideas evolve gradually out of older ones. On the contrary, really major advances in all sciences – including rock art research – tend to be rather sudden, and the new ideas are often altogether incompatible with the old ones. Scientists then have to take a clear-cut decision to abandon the old ways of doing research and of understanding the subject and to set out on a new voyage of discovery.

Science does not achieve these major advances by the gradual and painstaking accumulation of 'facts', important as that sort of work may be, but rather by devising radically new ways of understanding the facts. It is a bit like the well-known optical illusion that looks like a rabbit and then suddenly, at a blink, turns into a duck, the rabbit's ears becoming the duck's bill. In rock art research, paintings and engravings that for many years appeared quite obviously to depict, for instance, people dancing or animals standing in the veld, have suddenly turned out to be something quite different and far less simple when real San beliefs are taken into account. The difference between these transformations in rock art research and the optical illusion is that the more complex version was the artist's intention and the original, straightforward interpretation was a mistaken view, an illusion created by a Western way of looking at pictures. This book describes a number of such far-reaching and exciting trans-formations of our understanding – discoveries made right under our noses that have forced us to give up old approaches to the art or to develop them in new ways.

The optical illusion changes from a rabbit to a duck apparently without the viewer playing an active part in the transformation. Changes in scientific understanding are, of course, not like that: they are brought about by people and those people live in a world of pressures, culturally controlled values and, yes, personal ambitions. It would be wrong to suppose that rock art researchers are any more immune to these influences than, say, historians or sociologists. Try as they may, they are children of their own time, and their outlook is at least in some ways moulded by their social and intellectual environments. No scientists, not even rock art researchers, live in an ivory tower, where, isolated from the affairs of the world, they pursue 'pure' science – much as they may like to think so. That is why rock art researchers must try to be selfcritical, to examine long-held beliefs and to ask what (or whose) ideology these beliefs serve.

Are they really objective, 'scientific' explanations, or do some beliefs about the art actually project a view of the San that underwrites a particular political position, just as a way of recounting history can justify a group's political domination? Have books on rock art tended to support beliefs about the inevitability of Western power? Has the ideology of Western domination obscured the true nature of San rock art?

With these rather disturbing questions at the back of our minds, we shall, in this introductory chapter, concentrate on how the three most important ways of looking at southern African rock art started. We shall call these the aesthetic, the narrative and the interpretative approaches. In later chapters we shall examine each approach in more detail so that we can form some idea of their merits and limitations. In this way we shall be preparing ourselves for making our own discoveries in the painted rock shelters and on the open hilltops. There are many paintings and engravings out there waiting to be looked at with new eyes and with a better knowledge of the problems involved in understanding this ancient art.

One of the first people to try to understand southern African rock art was Sir John Barrow, who journeyed through the Cape Colony and beyond in 1797 and 1798. He was, naturally enough, excited to discover rock paintings and, like many writers after him, he described remote, almost inaccessible sites in somewhat exaggerated terms: 'The kloofs or chasms, washed by torrents of water rushing down the steep sides of the high stratified mountains, frequently leave a succession of caverns, of which the Bosjeman chooses the highest...' The paintings he found in these 'caverns' were so well done that he marvelled at their 'force and spirit' and that they could have been painted by a people whom the colonists regarded as 'Troops of abandon'd Wretches' lacking laws, fixed abodes and religion. The beauty of the art made Barrow think that the San had been rendered more 'savage ... by the conduct of the European settlers'. At this early time rock art was to some extent challenging the colonists' opinion of the San, and Barrow was one of the few who spoke out to defend the San against the false image that had been built up and, indeed, that has persisted right up to the present.

As for the paintings themselves, Barrow seems to have been almost exclusively concerned with their *aesthetic*, or artistic, aspects. He was, of course, assuming that the paintings, especially those of animals, were 'art' in the same sense that Westerners perceive 'art' and consequently that aesthetics and 'beauty' were high on the artists' own list of priorities. Whether he was right or wrong in this assessment, he discovered that the paintings are certainly not just crude daubings made by 'primitive savages', as most people of his time believed; they are beautiful and a source of great pleasure. This is the first way of looking at San rock art and, as we shall see in Chapter 2, it can lead to some delightful discoveries.

Another British knight, Sir James Alexander, developed Barrow's ideas. In 1835 Alexander was travelling in the vicinity of present-day Oudtshoorn. There he was taken to 'overhanging rocks in the most sequestered spots' where there were paintings. He included in the book he wrote three copies of these paintings made by his guide, Major C. C. Michell. Like Barrow, he was surprised to find that 'these rude attempts of uncivilized artists are not utterly devoid of merit'. But he went further than Barrow and his remarks take us on to the *narrative* approach.

Commenting on the first of Michell's copies, Alexander drew attention to the depiction of hunting bows. Curiously, he does seem to have been aware that the San, even at this time, were famous for their skill with bow and arrow. Alexander's observations on the second copy are more complex. He thought it represented 'an embassy of females suing for peace; or what may be a

A

Copies of southern Cape rock paintings made by Major C. C. Michell in 1835 for Sir James Alexander. A: Alexander drew attention to the bows. B: Alexander thought this painting depicted 'an embassy of females suing for peace'.

B

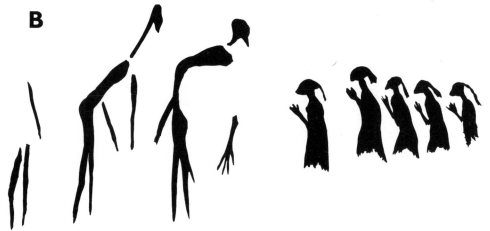

dance of females'. His confidence in his ability to 'read' the painting in this very detailed way is seen in his next remark. Favouring the diplomatic interpretation, he added, 'No one can deny that their reception is a gracious one, to judge by the polite attitudes of the male figures, perhaps chiefs.'

Although Alexander did not know it, he was initiating a very popular approach to southern African rock art. Since his time, there has been a long tradition of writers who have treated the art as a vivid record of an extinct, or all but extinct, way of life. For them, the art depicts the hunting techniques and weapons, the dress, rituals and customs of the Later Stone Age San. They feel they can discover in the art things about the artists that they cannot discover from archaeological excavations or the reports of travellers and anthropologists. One of the earliest and still one of the most influential writers in this tradition was the geologist George William Stow. In the 1860s he started making copies of rock paintings in the Orange Free State and the eastern Cape in the belief that he was compiling a narrative of 'the manners and customs of the Bushmen, as depicted by themselves'. This narrative included 'hunting scenes, dances, fightings, etc., showing the modes of warfare, the chase, weapons, disguises, etc.' We shall examine the *narrative* approach in Chapter 3.

The beginnings of the third approach, *interpretation*, appear in both Barrow's and Alexander's comments. Barrow was intrigued by painted 'crosses, circles, points and lines … placed in a long rank'. He thought they were 'intended to express some meaning', but he had no idea what that meaning could have been. Alexander faced the same problem

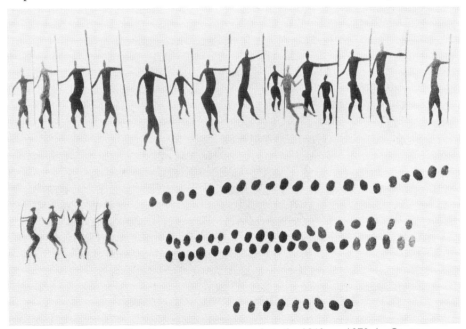

Copy of eastern Orange Free State rock paintings made in the 1860s or 1870s by George William Stow.

when he came to the painting in Major Michell's third copy. He remarked on the 'amphibious nature' of the figures, but in the end he had to admit, 'We are unable to assist the reader, even by a conjecture, in elucidating the meaning of that which he here sees represented.' Despite Alexander's bafflement, this has become one of the best-known and most debated of southern African rock paintings. It has been copied by many people and has appeared in a number of publications. As we shall see in Chapters 5 and 6, the successive interpretations of this painting illustrate the ways in which our knowledge of San rock art has developed over the years. But when, in 1835, Alexander tried to understand it, he could find nothing to say.

In many cases it is easy to admire the aesthetics of the art. Often, though not with Alexander's 'amphibious' painting, it is also easy to see what it apparently depicts – people, bows and arrows, animals, and so forth. It is much less easy to follow the third approach to rock art – to interpret what it meant to the artists and original viewers. Of course, once we have interpreted the art, we may have to go back and revise our opinion about what it actually depicts. This is what we do in Chapter 7 with a well-known painting.

To understand the distinction

C. C. Michell's copy of a puzzling southern Cape rock painting.

Leonardo da Vinci's *The Last Supper*.

between the aesthetic, the narrative and the interpretative approaches consider Leonardo da Vinci's famous mural painting, *The Last Supper*. This painting depicts thirteen men seated at a table. *Aesthetically*, we could admire the way in which Leonardo fitted the composition into the space available, the variety of attitudes in which the men are depicted, and the sense of movement. As *narrative*, the painting could be seen as a record of customs, table manners, dress and architecture. To move on to the *interpretative* level we should have to know the New Testament account of the Last Supper, Christian beliefs about Christ, and also something about Western artistic conventions. Then we should be able to analyse the various gestures and postures, each expressing a different reaction, as Christ speaks the words, 'One of you shall betray me.' Judas, for instance, is shown knocking over the salt – a symbol of impending

disaster – and he clutches a bag of money, the root of all evil. We should also learn that by choosing this subject for a wall in a monks' refectory Leonardo was extending the monks' every meal to include the drama of Christ's institution of the Eucharist. Most interesting of all, we should have to go back and change our mind about what it depicts because Christian beliefs show that this is no ordinary meal. Properly understood from the point of view of the artist and those for whom he painted, the picture does not depict thirteen ordinary men seated at a table enjoying an ordinary meal. One of them is not an ordinary man: even though he looks no different from the other men – no halo, no special clothes, no stigmata – he is divine (God and man at the same time) and he is instituting one of the most important Christian rituals. Without an understanding of Christianity, this is something we could never have guessed, no matter how long we pondered the picture.

Moving from one of these levels to the next is a journey of discovery: new shades of meaning appear, apparently mundane details, such as the spilling of the salt, are revealed as intensely symbolic, and we are drawn into the picture and all it means, as the monks of Leonardo's day must have been as they ate their daily supper. Close study affords handsome dividends. This is certainly true of San rock art. As, in the next chapters, we move from the aesthetic to the narrative and then on to the interpretative levels we shall be moving deeper into the complex experience that San artists depicted, and we shall discover that there is a great deal more to southern African rock art than Barrow and Alexander ever imagined.

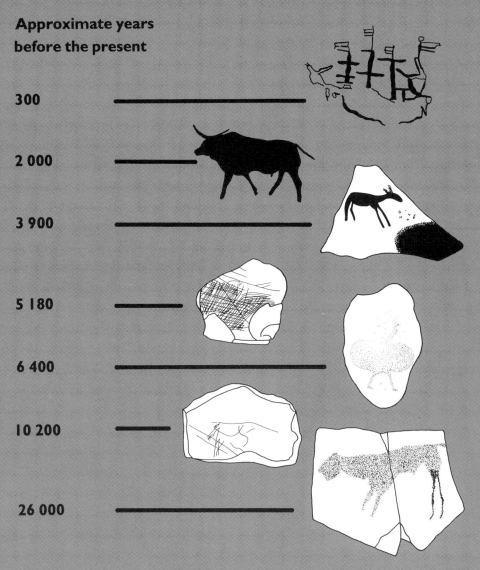

Approximate years before the present

300

2 000

3 900

5 180

6 400

10 200

26 000

DATED SOUTHERN AFRICAN ROCK ART. The oldest five examples, all done on portable stones, were dated by radiocarbon techniques performed on carbon found in the same layers as the stones. The next most recent example can be dated by the first appearance of cattle in southern Africa, in some parts as long as nearly 2 000 years ago, though the painting shown is probably much younger. The masts of the ship suggest a date in the second half of the seventeenth century (From top to bottom: after Johnson 1979: fig. 97; from the eastern Cape; after photograph by Binneman; after Humphreys and Thackeray 1983: fig. 43; after Thackeray 1983: fig. 1; after Humphreys and Thackeray 1983: fig. 43; after Wendt 1976: fig. 2).

2

The aesthetic approach

San rock art is immediately attractive to most Westerners. The delicate features of many paintings and the sure, economical lines of many engravings are breathtaking. Simply looking at the art gives a great deal of pleasure. It is therefore not surprising that San rock art has had a considerable influence on many southern African artists who come from a Western background. Some, like Walter Battiss, one of the pioneering students of southern African rock art, Robert Slingsby and Pippa Skotnes consciously use San forms and ideas, while the work of others reflects these forms and ideas even though the artists themselves do not explicitly lay claim to their influence.

From an aesthetic point of view, it is the depictions of animals that have

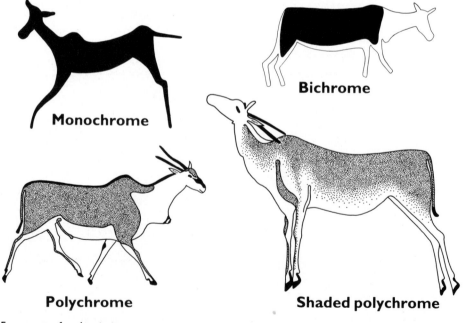

Monochrome

Bichrome

Polychrome

Shaded polychrome

Four types of rock paintings.

attracted the most comment and praise. The reasons for this are obvious. First, they are painted and engraved in striking detail. When looking at a polychrome painting of an eland, for instance, one should note small details such as the tuft of red hair on its forehead, the black line along the back, the darkening of the snout, the cloven hoofs, and the way in which the shading moulds the contours of the body. Even monochrome depictions often accurately show the form of an eland's leg, fetlocks, tufted tail and so forth. The way in which San artists achieved such fine detail on comparatively rough rock faces is amazing. Engravings too show many of these details, especially the folds of skin on an eland's shoulders and, sometimes, facial features and the twist of the horns. As many writers have remarked, the San were keen observers of the world around them.

In addition to having so many realistic details, depictions of animals are skilfully rendered in a variety of postures. Most common is the side view, but antelope, especially eland, are also painted as seen from the front, from the back, and, occasionally, from above. Sometimes an animal is shown with its head turned. Others are painted lying down, running or leaping – in fact in every conceivable position.

Paintings of human figures are

A

B

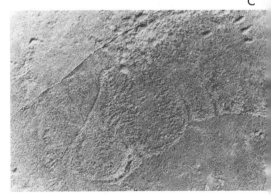

C

Three kinds of rock engravings. A: Scraped engraving of an eland (Cape). B: Incised engraving of an eland (Transvaal). C: Pecked engraving of a hippopotamus head (western Transvaal) (Photographs and rubbing: T. A. Dowson).

similarly detailed and animated. They
sometimes show fingers, toes and even
facial features, though these are
comparatively rare. In polychrome
paintings there are often bands at the
wrist, waist, knee and ankle that may
depict ostrich eggshell beads or leather
bands. In addition, they show features
of dress and headgear. The human
figure appears less frequently among
the rock engravings and, when it does,
it is generally represented more
schematically.

As with animal depictions, human
figures are shown in a variety of
postures, such as standing, walking,
running, lying down, sitting and
dancing. Some figures are drawn with
their legs outstretched, almost as if
they are flying across the rock face.
Animation is indeed one of the chief
impressions conveyed by San rock art.

Rock paintings of human beings in various postures.

Rock engraving of human beings (Photograph: T. A. Dowson).

All these features of animal and human depictions teach us an important lesson: if we want to discover anything about the art, both paintings and engravings should be examined closely, not viewed from a distance. Unlike the custom with some Western art, the viewer should be as close to the depiction as the artist was when he or she made it. Only then can it be fully appreciated.

Close examination also raises some controversial points about the aesthetics of San rock art. For instance, some writers have claimed that San artists occasionally used perspective. Those who consider the San 'primitive' believe the artists were struggling, but for the most part failing, to achieve 'correct' perspective, as if the sort of perspective we see in many Western pictures is the pinnacle of artistic achievement. There are, however, different kinds of perspective of which the sort used in much Western art since the Renaissance is only one: a glance at Chinese paintings shows that there is no such thing as 'correct' perspective. The kind used by most Western artists is constructed on the principle of lines converging on a distant vanishing point so that objects farther away from the viewer are depicted smaller. Despite claims to the contrary, it is doubtful if the San used this technique. If they did, it appears so seldom that one would have to conclude that it did not play a prominent part in their repertoire of skills.

Another controversial point is superpositioning. One often encounters paintings (and, less often, engravings) that have been done directly on top of others. One opinion about this is that San artists simply ignored the work of their predecessors, but there are a number of points that challenge this explanation.

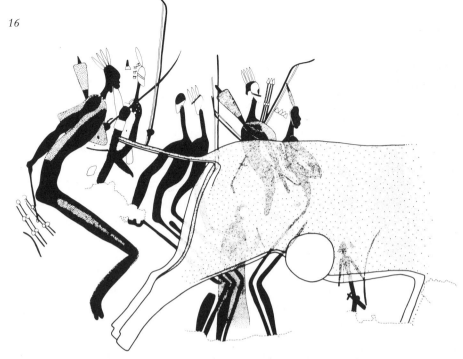

Rock painting of an eland superimposed on dancers (eastern Orange Free State).

Eland superimposed on other eland (eastern Cape) (Photograph: T. A. Dowson).

In the first place, there are many cases where there is ample open space to accommodate a second depiction; yet it is directly on top of an earlier one. Secondly, statistical analyses have shown that certain combinations of subject matter in superpositioning were avoided while others were favoured. In the Drakensberg, for example, eland are frequently painted on top of other eland or human figures, but human figures are seldom painted on eland. The reason for this preference is unknown. Lastly and perhaps most persuasively, there are cases of contrived superpositioning in which an artist painted the second depiction in two parts to give the impression that it is underneath the first one. Clearly, in these cases, the artist wanted not just superpositioning but a specific combination: it was not good enough for the second painting to be done next to or on top of the first; it had to be 'beneath' it.

A number of researchers have used superpositioning to construct stylistic sequences. The supposed order of the successive styles through time is established by noting which lies beneath which. At one time it was thought that two major periods could be established by this method and by noting the subject matter of the art: a Pre-Bantu Period and a Post-Bantu Period. (Today 'Bantu' is used only in a linguistic sense, as in the phrase 'Bantu-speakers'.) Each of these

periods, so it was believed, could be divided into a number of phases. Taken together, the sequence of periods and phases showed a development from simple monochrome paintings to elaborate shaded polychromes and then a falling off into what was considered a crude or 'degenerate' art. The great divide between the so-called Pre-Bantu and Post-Bantu was often placed at about A.D. 1650.

Very little of this is accepted today. The concept of an inexorable cyclic 'rise and fall' of an art or a civilisation

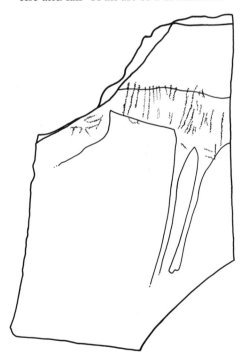

Painting of an animal done in two colours. Dated to between 19 000 and 27 000 years before the present (after Wendt 1976: fig. 3).

Antelope are the most commonly depicted animals. Other creatures, such as these, are less frequently depicted.

was derived from a philosophy of history that has been abandoned. It is better to see history as a long line and to seek reasons for the changes that occur along that line. In any event, the painted stones that Erich Wendt excavated in the Apollo 11 cave in southern Namibia show that two colours were being used by painters at least 19 000 years ago and very probably as much as 27 000 years ago.

Nor did the division of the art into major periods stand up to research. To understand why this scheme is no longer accepted we must first see how the periods were characterised. Professor C. van Riet Lowe, Director of the Archaeological Survey that was established in South Africa in 1935 largely through the influence of

General J. C. Smuts, described the Pre-Bantu Period thus: 'Pre-Bantu art is restful in the sense that it seems to have been enjoyed by people who had little, if anything, to fear and knew how to use their leisure... They were obviously a care-free and happy people with a fine sense of humour and caricature.' By contrast, the Post-Bantu Period included shields, spears and domestic animals and was characterised by a 'feeling of restlessness and lack of leisure... The peace they had formerly enjoyed was disrupted and their art suffered accordingly.'

The steps of this argument need to be examined critically. First, in the absence of any method for directly dating individual paintings on the walls of rock shelters, the supposed 'restlessness' and poor quality of certain paintings are ascribed – for no good reason – to the arrival of black farmers. Then the argument is put into reverse, and paintings are dated to the period following the arrival of the farmers because some are 'restless' and some are, in the opinion of the researcher, poorly done. Apart from the rather obvious point that paintings depicting shields and cattle must have been made after people with those things became known to the artists, the argument is circular.

The stylistic evolution of San rock art was thus believed to turn on the comparatively recent arrival of Bantu-speaking people. Despite all the research that has shown conclusively that Bantu-speaking farmers were in southern Africa nearly 2000 years ago, the fiction that they were immigrants at about the same time as the Europeans settled at the Cape persists even today because it is politically expedient to show that they do not have a prior claim to the land. Moreover, the black farmers are presented as usurpers who attacked and destroyed the peaceful San and, by implication, then turned their wrath against the equally peace-loving white colonists and destroyed their tranquillity too. In the supposed conflict between the San and the black farmers, the San are presented as helpless, simple folk who loved

dancing and used their leisure in the unhurried production of 'art'. As van Riet Lowe puts it, 'the artists, armed *only* with bows and arrows, and the

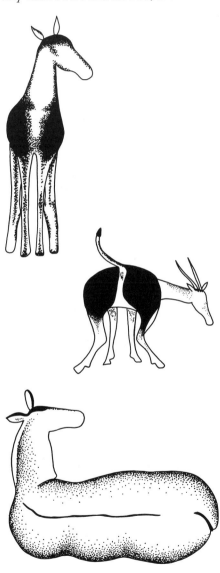

Antelope painted in different ways.

invaders armed with shields and spears' (emphasis added). In fact we know that, although there were no doubt clashes especially in the early years of contact, the San and the black farmers settled down to a reasonably amicable coexistence. Sometimes the San worked for the farmers and conducted rain-making ceremonies for them. Trade flourished between the two peoples. There was also intermarriage and, in times of stress, some farmers abandoned their fields and went to live with the San. There is absolutely no reason why the so-called 'restful' paintings could not have been made right up to the end of the nineteenth century.

This is one of the clearest cases of rock art writers being, wittingly or unwittingly, the instruments of a dominant colonial ideology. Rock art research on styles and periods was harnessed to propagate a false history in which blacks are the principal aggressors and the San are helpless 'children' who, in the very nature of things, could not survive.

In the past the construction of stylistic sequences like this was a substantial part of southern African rock art research, but this is not the

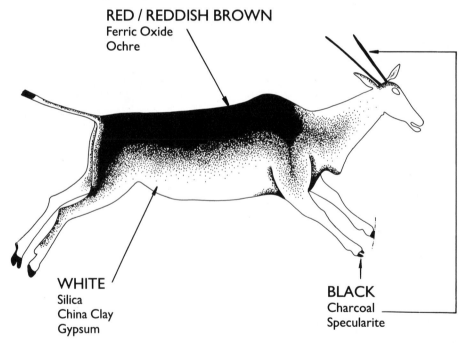

RED / REDDISH BROWN
Ferric Oxide
Ochre

WHITE
Silica
China Clay
Gypsum

BLACK
Charcoal
Specularite

Pigments were mixed with fat, blood or, possibly, water

Paints used by the San.

case today. Researchers now recognise how difficult it is to define a sequence of styles objectively so that anyone, having read the description, can sort the paintings in a shelter into the 'correct' sequence. Words like 'crude', 'degenerate', 'of fine style', 'elegant' and so forth are far too subjective to be useful in defining styles. After all, one person's 'crude' painting is another's Picasso! The fact that a painting may appear to us crude or hastily done does not imply that the painter was lacking the necessary skills. He or she may have intended it to look that way in order to convey a message that differed from the message of more detailed and delicate paintings. Moreover, as A. R. Willcox found in the Drakensberg, all too often a sequence established in one shelter is contradicted in the next. It is not surprising that 'style' as a tool in rock art research is too vague; much more work needs to be done on this problem because we do not know all the conventions of San art. Some researchers go so far as to say that, whatever its relevance in the study of Western art, 'style' is valueless in rock art research, but this may be too extreme a view.

Despite the reservations one may have about perspective, style, periods and other matters, there is no doubt that San rock art is highly sophisticated. Today few would agree with those writers who describe it as simple stick figures. Perhaps that opinion arises from the false belief that the San in some way preserved humankind's innocent infancy.

The sophistication of San rock art is indeed a source of wonder: few modern viewers can fail to be captivated by it. But even as we start to discover and evaluate its finer aesthetic points, we come up against the sobering thought that we are doing so from a Western, not from a San, point of view. We have to remember that we are taking an outsider's view. Even with the closest examination and the most sensitive response the aesthetic approach does not, *by itself*, take us to the heart of the matter. How much diminished our appreciation of *The Last Supper* would be if we did not know what it depicted: we would be left with meaningless description and praise. So too with San rock art. Without wishing in any way to belittle the very real aesthetic delight the art affords, we must move on from admiration to understanding.

3

The narrative approach

The next problem is to answer the question: If San rock art is narrative, just what does it depict? This may seem a naive question because it is quite obvious what the art depicts – animals and people. But it is the apparent simplicity of the question that can easily trip us up.

Sir John Barrow, Sir James Alexander and especially George Stow tried to see something of the daily experience of the artists in their work. It is, after all, reasonable to suppose that the sort of life they lived would find its way in some measure into their pictures. Unfortunately, these earlier writers did not know much about that way of life. Today, thanks to the work of many anthropologists and archaeologists, we know a great deal about the San.

They were Later Stone Age people and lived what anthropologists call a hunter-gatherer, or foraging, way of life. It is common to find them presented as living, until very recently, in a kind of Garden of Eden, isolated from outside influences – the so-called Lost World of the Kalahari. Recent research has shown that this was not the case. As John Parkington of the University of Cape Town says, 'We know now ... that all hunter-gatherers in southern Africa have shared the landscape for at least 1 500 years with pastoralists or agriculturalists.' The Kalahari was never 'lost'. We should not think of the San as 'hunter-gatherers' in the sense that, isolated from other peoples, they subsisted by hunting and gathering only, but in the sense that, unlike their neighbours, their society was organised on the principles of communal ownership of land and resources, sharing, and a political system that had no chiefs or ruling elite.

Still, like all foragers, the men concerned themselves principally with hunting animals and the women with gathering plant foods. Both these activities appear in the art.

Contrary to a widespread belief, actual hunting scenes are comparatively rare. In the Ndedema Gorge, Harald Pager found only 29 hunting scenes in a total of 2 860 individual paintings of human beings and animals. A closer look at these 29 scenes led to an unexpected discovery: only 7 show men shooting at game,

A Drakensberg rock painting of a man carrying a bow, arrows and a quiver.

put his quiver on' – in other words, he has gone hunting. Depictions of men with quivers, hunting bags and, of course, bows and arrows may therefore imply hunting even though an animal is not shown.

This hunting equipment is skilfully made and used. San bows are light and do not shoot an arrow with enough force to kill an animal on impact. Instead the San rely on poison obtained from plants and from the grub of a beetle. It is placed just behind the point so as not to blunt it. They throw away the meat around an arrow wound, but the rest of the animal is edible. Nevertheless, the poison is highly toxic if it enters the bloodstream directly, and even a slight wound from a poisoned arrow is fatal to a human being. To ensure the poison has its effect on a large animal, San arrows are made on the link-shaft principle. Each arrow consists of a reed shaft, a torpedo-shaped link, a short collar and the point. When an arrow strikes an animal, the impact forces the link into the collar and splits

and there is only one wounded animal. In contrast, 11 hunting scenes show men running after but not actually killing game. The importance of these results is that, whilst it is true that hunting is depicted, the activity does not appear quite as often as one would expect for a society that depended to a large extent on meat for its daily food.

Hunting is, however, more subtly implied by the equipment men carry. San hunters keep their arrows in a tubular quiver made from bark, and they often carry this in a hunting bag. When a San person enquires where a man is, he or she may be told, 'He has

Eastern Orange Free State rock painting of a man apparently hunting antelope. Note that he has a hand raised to his face. See pages 30 and 54 for an explanation of this gesture.

Western Cape rock painting of a man holding a triple-curved bow (after T. Johnson 1979: pl. 73).

it. The shaft then falls away and the poisoned point remains firmly embedded in the animal. Close examination of paintings often reveals that the sections of link-shaft arrows have been depicted with different colours.

John Parkington and his colleagues have argued that triple-curved bows, a type not recorded by early travellers or anthropologists, are depicted in the western Cape. The triple-curved bow is more powerful than a single-curved bow and can deliver an arrow with sufficient power to kill an animal. Arrows used with such a bow would, of course, have to be more robust than the link-shaft ones used by San hunters today.

The same researchers have suggested another, completely different hunting technique that, like the triple-curved bow, is not noted in the historical record. Some paintings in the Cedarberg show criss-crossed forms that look like nets. Often animals are depicted in such a way that they appear to be running into the 'nets'. We know that the San had the technology to make netting for carrying ostrich eggshells and so forth. It is possible that they also made larger nets into which small antelope could be driven. Along the Limpopo River there are numerous paintings of another kind of trap: they seem to depict conical baskets made for catching fish.

The animals the San hunted by these techniques and by snaring are depicted in the art, but, as is so often the case, close study turns up puzzling features. For some years it was thought that the San were painting a kind of menu – in other words, the animals they hunted and ate. Some writers went further and suggested that the depictions may have been a magical way of ensuring good hunting. One of the problems with this view is that the San do not, as far as we know, believe in that kind of

magic. Another is the fact that the animals depicted are not representative of San diet, as Tim Maggs showed in the Western Province and Pat Vinnicombe in the Drakensberg: small animals caught by snaring account for most of their meat. Nor are the painted animals representative of the species found in the vicinity of the sites. In many areas of southern Africa, eland are 'over represented' in the art, while other species which the San ate, such as wildebeest, are never or hardly ever depicted. It follows that, if the art is a

Rock painting from the Limpopo Valley depicting a fish trap (after H. Pager 1975: fig. 3).

narrative, it is not a simple, straightforward narrative of the animal world the San saw around them.

This kind of skewed version of the 'real' world is also reflected in another anomaly. Hunters supply about 40 per cent of the people's food, while the women's plant foods constitute about 60 per cent. Despite the importance of the women's contribution, they are depicted comparatively seldom. For instance, amongst 802 human figures in the Giant's Castle area of the Natal Drakensberg, 252 can be identified as male by primary sexual charac-teristics or by the fact that they carry bows and arrows. By contrast, only 18 can be identified as female. Again, it seems that, although such real things as bows and arrows are depicted, the art is not a simple, straightforward narrative of San life. Certainly, the art

Eastern Orange Free State rock painting of women holding digging sticks weighted with bored stones.

is not a 'picture' of food and ways of getting food.

When women are depicted, they are often holding digging sticks. Close examination of these sticks sometimes reveals that they have a round shape about half-way along their length. These blobs represent bored stones which were fixed to the sticks with wooden wedges. The stones gave extra weight and made digging in hard ground easier. Bored stones are found in many parts of southern Africa, but they are not used by the Kalahari San.

The women's task of gathering plant foods is possibly the chief factor affecting San mobility. After a while of camping at one spot, the women begin to complain that they have to walk too far to find food. The time has come to move on. These moves are all carefully planned; there is no aimless wandering. The San are nomadic only in the sense that they move to areas that they know will have certain kinds of food at different times of the year. Each group follows an annual round that ensures an adequate food supply.

At certain times of the year, when the food and water in a given area allow it, a number of small groups amalgamate. They enjoy these larger social occasions when they learn news of distant relatives, arrange marriages and perform large trance, or curing, dances. To what extent are these contrasting group sizes depicted in the art? There is no doubt that the art depicts large and small groups of people, but it is difficult to correlate these with counts of actual San groups as they exist – or existed – in the Kalahari and with the accounts of early travellers. Working in the western Cape, Tim Maggs found that a distinct kind of painting showing a seated group with bags above them had an average of about thirteen individuals, whereas ordinary standing and walking groups had an average of about only seven individuals. He concluded that the distinctive seated groups may have some correlation with the actual size of San groups in that area and that the paintings may express feelings of group unity. Further comparison of other painted groups with counts made of actual San groups suggests that thirteen is fewer than the 20-24 individuals reported for the Kalahari San. Still less correlation between actual and painted groups is implied by Harald Pager's work in the Ndedema Gorge in the Natal Drakensberg. He found that there is a generally steady decline in frequency from groups of two individuals (157 examples) to groups of three (83 examples) to groups of nine (only 9 examples), and so on. It is not possible to distinguish two distinct group sizes. Again we conclude that, although the art does seem to depict a few daily activities, it would be wrong to regard it as an accurate record from

which we can 'read off' facts about the sort of lives the artists and their fellows lived, as George Stow believed he could from the copies he made in the 1870s.

This research on group size is based on comparisons between the art and recorded San groups, and introduces a principle of southern African rock art research that is described in more detail in the following chapters. Here we apply it to one specific kind of painting and activity – the trance dance. In doing so we shall see that, as with hunting, the role of women and group sizes, the art is narrative in a

A San woman demonstrating the use of a weighted digging stick, Cape Town, 1884 (Bleek and Lloyd Collection, University of Cape Town).

restricted way only. But, more importantly, our examination of how trance dancing is depicted will lead us on, in the following chapters, to some idea of the filter through which daily life passed before it was taken up into the art. The trance dance is the San's most important religious ritual, and an understanding of its various features and purpose is essential to a proper appreciation of the rock art.

The San perform the trance dance most frequently when there are large numbers of people present, though they may go into trance at other times as well. At one of the large dances in the Kalahari today the women sit in a circle around a fire as they clap the rhythm and sing special medicine songs. They believe these songs are imbued with a supernatural potency. This potency, which comes ultimately from God himself, is also in the stomachs of the medicine people, or shamans as they are called in the anthropological literature. A shaman is a ritual specialist who goes into a state of altered consciousness (generally known as trance) to heal people, change the weather and so forth. San shamans constitute, on average, about half the men in any group; about a third of the older women are also shamans.

As a trance dance increases in intensity, the women's clapping and singing combine with the men's insistent dancing to cause the potency to 'boil', as they put it, and to rise up the shamans' spines. When it 'explodes' in their heads, they enter trance. For them, trance is the spirit world, and in this dimension they heal the sick, remonstrate with malevolent spirits, go on out-of-body journeys and even confront God. The

A Drakensberg rock painting of a trance dance; seated women clap while men dance facing them (Original in Local History Museum, Durban).

San performing a trance dance in the Kalahari in the 1950s (Photograph: Lorna Marshall).

now-extinct southern San also believed the shamans could make rain and guide antelope herds into the hunters' ambush.

The southern people varied the form of the dance: sometimes the shamans (or a single shaman) danced in the centre while the women stood around them. The missionaries Thomas Arbousset and François Daumas, who came to southern Africa in 1836, described one of these dances as it was performed in what is now Lesotho:

The movement consists of irregular jumps; it is as if one saw a herd of calves leaping, to use a native comparison. They gambol together till all are fatigued and covered with perspiration. The thousand cries which they raise, and the exertions which they make, are so violent that it is not unusual to see some one sink to the ground exhausted and covered with blood, which pours from the nostrils; it is on this account that this dance is called *mokoma*, or the dance of *blood*.

The missionaries added that these dances lasted all night – as they still do in the Kalahari – and that the San 'worshipped' /Kaggen, their trickster-god, in the dance.

Certain features of this 'dance of blood' are faithfully depicted in the art. One of the most important is the blood that flows from the noses of the shamans when they enter trance. Sometimes people are depicted with a hand raised to the nose. Another feature is a bending-forward posture that can become so acute that dancers have to support their weight on sticks. The Kalahari San ascribe this position to the painful contraction of their stomach muscles. The posture is sometimes accompanied by a stretching back of the arms; the shamans say they do this when they ask God to put more potency into their spines. In some of the more highly detailed paintings the men are wearing dancing rattles made from cocoons or dried springbok ears and filled with small stones or pieces of

A Natal Drakensberg rock painting of a man playing a musical bow.

ostrich eggshell.

Today these rattles are the only musical instruments closely associated with the trance dance, but there is evidence that another instrument, the musical bow, was played by shamans in the past. The San musical bow is an ordinary hunting bow which is tapped with a stick. Holding the bow more or less horizontally, a player may use his mouth as a resonator. When the stave is held vertically or semi-vertically, some performers like to use a calabash or other object as a resonator and so produce more varied sounds. The resonator can be gripped in the left hand and pressed against the stave, or held between the stave and the stomach, or placed on the ground with the farther end of the bow resting on it. When the bow is played with the resonator on the ground, the nearer end of the bow is cradled against the left shoulder. The stopping of the string to produce notes of varying pitch is achieved by placing the chin against the string. About half-a-dozen rock paintings of people playing bows in this manner have been found.

The sound produced by a San musician is poignantly evocative, almost hypnotic. Elizabeth Marshall Thomas describes it thus:

We stopped to listen, caught in the net of music which Ukxone had cast into the air, for it was a soft, sad song in a minor key to wring your heart, to make you think of places far away and make you feel like crying.

/Kaunu, a nineteenth-century San shaman who played this sort of music to call up the rain, was said to have eyes that shone like a beast of prey's eyes. While everyone was asleep, he used to 'strike the bowstring'. When the people awoke, 'the clouds had shut in the place'.

Another artefact that is closely associated with the shamans and that is depicted is the flywhisk. Dancers use flywhisks to extract invisible 'arrows of sickness' that may be in people and also, so they say, simply because it gives a pleasant feeling to dance with a whisk. Certain shamans who

specialised in game control also wore caps with antelope ears sewn so that they stood up. They believed the antelope would follow the wearer of such a cap.

This notion of guiding the movements of antelope introduces a 'non-real' element that is highly developed in many paintings. Sometimes a trance dancer has a long line, far too long to be a feather, coming from the top of his head. In other paintings the human figures have antelope heads. These heads were formerly thought to depict masks, but the most detailed examples show that the whole head is that of an antelope. Moreover, these figures

A San man playing a musical bow (Photograph: Lorna Marshall).

often have antelope hoofs and hair growing on their bodies. All these features call in question the belief that paintings of dances are *just* a narrative record of daily life. Certainly, the trance dance is depicted with great attention to realistic detail, but, as with other activities, there are also features that cannot be easily explained.

All these features, both real and non-real, are indicators of trance performance, but, in addition to being included in paintings of large dances, where one would expect to find them, they appear with isolated human figures or with people who seem to be simply walking, standing or sitting. This, as we shall see later, is a vital clue to the overall meaning of the art, but for the moment we need only note, once again, that aspects of the real world are clearly depicted in the art – but somehow altered. The art is narrative only up to a point.

Nevertheless, it is fascinating to discover these narrative elements in San rock art. In this short book I have been able to mention only a few, but the more detailed books listed at the end describe many more. At the same time it must be emphasised that it is

Rock paintings depicting various dancing postures. A: Eastern Orange Free State. B: Eastern Cape.

unwise to treat the art as if it were merely a series of literal photographs of what actually happened in a San camp. If we wish to infer aspects of daily life solely from the art, we have to exercise great care and do so only from a deep background knowledge of the San.

'What does San rock art depict?', the question we asked at the beginning of this chapter, is really a rather naive question that presupposes a naive answer because it directs our attention to the superficial appearances of the art. We could easily end up by answering, 'People and animals', and thus miss the rather odd biases and features we have been noting. If we asked the same question about *The Last Supper*, we could make the mistake of replying, 'A table, a cloth, some men, plates, and so on', and thus miss the point of the picture. Perhaps we should rather ask, 'In what *sense* – if any – is San rock art narrative?' In the following chapters we shall see that this question does not have a simple answer. As we found with *The Last Supper* and Christianity, an understanding of what San rock art depicts is intimately bound up with interpreting it in terms of San beliefs.

Eastern Cape rock painting of a man holding a flywhisk and running along a 'non-real' red line fringed with white dots; two long lines emanate from his head.

4

Rediscovering the San

In recent years our whole understanding of the art has changed, and we have been able to go on from where Sir James Alexander, Sir John Barrow and George Stow left off. Alexander was baffled by the curious mermaid-like figures and the extremely elongated but apparently human figure between them, and Barrow could not explain the 'crosses, circles, points and lines … placed in a long rank'. The paintings they were looking at are of two kinds that we may very loosely define as representational (recognisable, if distorted, depictions of human beings and animals) and geometric (dots, crosses, zigzags and so forth). To find out how researchers tackled the interpretative problems posed by these two kinds of painting and the ways in which they may be related to each other, we take up the tale of southern African rock art research where we left it at the end of Chapter 1. It is one of archaeology's detective stories.

Barrow's and Alexander's approach was typical of their time, and there was not much change in people's interest in rock art for some decades. People hoped that the 'Bushman problem' would be resolved by extermination and by forcing the survivors to work for white farmers. Highlighting the beauty of their art would have been counterproductive to maintaining the fiction that, as one of the 'lower races', they were little better than animals and consequently had no right to the land they inhabited. Then circumstances that had nothing to do with rock art brought about the most important events in the whole history of the study. In 1873 the Hlubi chief Langalibalele was reluctant to register guns his people had acquired because he realised the demand was an attempt to weaken his position. Knowing from bitter experience that his refusal would bring retribution, he withdrew from Natal into what is now Lesotho. The Natal government called on Joseph Millerd Orpen, a magistrate in the north-eastern Cape, to go into the mountains and try to head off Langalibalele. While his forces were being assembled, Orpen secured the services of a young San guide named Qing, who 'had never seen a white man but in fighting'. Nevertheless, Orpen won his confidence and later

J. M. Orpen who recorded rock paintings and San beliefs in 1873 (Cullen Library, University of the Witwatersrand).

wrote, 'When happy and at ease smoking over camp fires, I got from him … stories and explanations of paintings, some of which he showed and I copied on our route.'

Orpen sent his copies of the paintings and Qing's explanations of them to the *Cape Monthly Magazine* in Cape Town. The editor at once took them to Wilhelm Bleek, a German linguist who was working with San people from the Kenhardt area. Bleek and his sister-in-law, Lucy Lloyd, then obtained further comments on the paintings from these people. The great importance of these events is that Orpen and Bleek sought the San's own understanding of the paintings. Unlike their predecessors and

contemporaries, they did not for one moment suppose that they could simply look at the paintings and intuitively know what they were about. Bleek and Lloyd also had access to other copies of San paintings, notably some of those made by Stow in his attempt to compile a 'history' of the San, but, in trying to understand the paintings, they always kept as close as possible to authentic San beliefs and explanations. As a result, Orpen and the Bleek family came to realise that there was much more to the art than the simple animals and people it appeared to depict. Bleek went so far as to use the word 'religious' when writing about the ideas expressed in the art. This must have seemed a bit excessive to those who claimed the San were so 'primitive' that they had no religion at all. By insisting on the religious nature of the art Bleek was in fact openly challenging many people who were trying to dehumanise the San and so justify their subjugation and even extermination.

Bleek's view of the San was unusually enlightened for his time. Not only did he have San people living at his Cape Town home, but he was also a close friend of Bishop Colenso, a liberal clergyman, who believed that God is in all people, even those who are not Christians. Today this does not sound an exceptional opinion, but in 1863 Colenso was tried by a church court for heresy. Wilhelm Bleek represented Colenso at the trial in Cape Town because the bishop refused to appear. The spirit of the time can be gauged from the verdict: Colenso was found guilty. This unfortunate outcome did not deter Bleek. He knew that he and Orpen had found some of the most important clues in the 'detective story' of San rock art and that those clues pointed to the essentially religious nature of the art, whatever others might think.

Unfortunately, this brave start did not develop into the kind of study it should have done. After Bleek's untimely death in 1875, the racist views that had led to Colenso's conviction triumphed, and it was many decades before the value of Orpen's and Bleek's clues was at all widely recognised. Instead of going forward, rock art research entered a retrogressive period during which Qing and the other San people were pushed from centre stage. Despite the cautionary example of Qing's complex interpretations of the paintings he showed Orpen, researchers continued to think, in the colonial manner, that any intelligent Westerner could look at the art and then sense intuitively what it depicted: for them there was really no need to ask the San what they themselves believed about their art.

Something of this trend can be seen even in the work of the Bleek family.

/Han≠kass'o, one of Wilhelm Bleek's and Lucy Lloyd's Cape San (Bleek and Lloyd Collection, University of Cape Town).

In 1911 Lucy Lloyd published *Specimens of Bushman Folklore*, a selection of the material she and her brother-in-law had taken down in the 1870s. The title of the book and the care with which it was prepared reflect the 'scientific' approach they cultivated, but their sensitivity to the San as people always shines through. For instance, Lloyd noted that //Kabbo, perhaps their best helper and teacher, 'much enjoyed the thought that the Bushman stories would become known by means of books'. But by the 1920s a new element began to show itself in the writing of

A group of Cape San photographed at the Breakwater Convict Station, Cape Town, about 1871 (Bleek and Lloyd Collection, University of Cape Town).

Wilhelm Bleek's daughter, Dorothea, who continued the work after Lloyd's death in 1914. We must remember that she was only two years old when her father died and that she lived through a time during which racial attitudes hardened. Moreover, when she unsuccessfully tried to trace the descendants of the San people who had lived with her family in Cape Town, she found only scattered groups of pathetic, impoverished people. Perhaps these circumstances led her to express opinions that contrast starkly with those of her father. She disparagingly laid great emphasis on the San's 'carefree, idle life' and the time they spent 'lounging about, watching bird and beast, and talking – always talking'. When in 1923 she published a collection of myths about /Kaggen, the southern San trickster-deity, she called it *The Mantis and His Friends*, a title that seems to suggest a child's story book and contrasts with the title chosen by Lloyd for her book. In her introduction Dorothea described the San thus: 'He remains all his life a child, averse to work, fond of play, of painting, singing, dancing, dressing up and acting, above all things fond of hearing and telling stories.' She seems to have succumbed to the colonial belief that all indigenous people, especially the San, are inherently lazy. The so-called 'laziness' is, however, a viable strategy, developed in response to their loss of traditional land-rights and being forced into a wage economy that marginalises them and ensures their continued poverty.

When she wrote about rock art this attitude to the San and the growing South African emphasis on race again asserted themselves. She considered the questions 'What race or races produced the artists?' and 'What race or races have the physical and cultural characteristics depicted?' to be central issues. So persistent was this theme that half a century later an overseas reviewer was to remark of a South African rock art book that the author had an 'obsession' with race. In the light of such attitudes, it is not surprising that in her *Survey of Our Present Knowledge of Rock Paintings in South Africa*, published in 1932, Dorothea Bleek had little to say about the meaning of the art. Despite her familiarity with the beliefs and customs collected by her father and her aunt, the nearest she came to interpretation was to remark in passing that 'one or two rock paintings may have something to do' with myth. For the rest, the meaning was evident upon inspection: a painting of an eland meant no more than 'This is an eland'.

In 1968 A. R. Willcox used the same title as Dorothea Bleek to survey the progress made in the intervening 34 years. Like Dorothea, he did not go beyond distribution, associated stone artefacts and the age of the art. He found, quite rightly, that 'What can be added now to Dorothea Bleek's summary ... is in some respects disappointing' and, more alarmingly, that the 'outlook for progress in this branch of archaeology is not very encouraging'.

On the other hand, it would be wrong to suppose that no useful work was done during this period. In fact many people continued to record the art, and there are large collections of copies made by such enthusiasts as the Abbé Henri Breuil, Helen Tongue, George Stow, members of the Frobenius expedition, and Walter Battiss. Unfortunately, most of these copies are, by today's standards, somewhat inaccurate. The early recorders missed details (or recorded features that do not exist), rearranged paintings to fit a page and, most damaging of all, selected paintings and engravings that interested them. What can one now say about, for instance, two eland beautifully reproduced in delicate watercolour when one knows that all the adjacent paintings have been omitted? A student would not be able to write a very good essay on *The Last Supper* if the copy from which he or she was working showed only two people seated at the table.

That is why these collections are of historical rather than scientific value. But, because they and their compilers kept the art in the public's imagination, they did make a valuable contribution; some of the copies are works of art in their own right.

We must remember that these early copies were made in the aesthetic and the narrative traditions. The idea that the art was made by real people with, as Wilhelm Bleek found, a highly developed religion does not seem to have occurred to most of the researchers of this time. Some went so far as to argue that the paintings and engravings should be studied, not as images that communicated ideas, but by the same techniques that had been devised for studying stone artefacts. In other words, they should be treated as lifeless objects. Like the San themselves, the art was dehumanised.

In contrast to this rather dismal period, the San are today once more centre stage. Just how this major and comparatively recent shift back to the actual creators of the art took place is interesting: the cause of the whole radical change, like Orpen's and Bleek's finding of the first clues, again lay outside of mainstream rock art research.

In the 1960s it was felt that no subject could call itself 'scientific' if it did not deal in numbers: tables, graphs and statistics became the order of the day. Rock art researchers saw these developments in other areas of scientific work and realised that, if their work was to become scientifically 'respectable', they too would have to move away from mere description to precise numerical statements. If we were to select one year as the turning point for rock art studies, it would be 1967. It was then that Patricia Vinnicombe published her seminal paper on the quantification of rock art. She urged that southern African rock art be recorded as objectively and as comprehensively as possible and, most important, that it be recorded numerically and thus be amenable to statistical analysis. Vinnicombe believed that Alexander, Stow and many of her own contemporaries had been too selective in their approach to the art: they had chosen only the most attractive paintings. Also in 1967, Tim Maggs, who had been working quite independently, published his numerical analysis of rock art from an area in the western Cape and thereby showed that quantitative methods could reveal highly significant aspects of the art.

Gone was the 'traditional' way of doing rock art research. Fanciful story-spinning around selected paintings was, at a stroke, a thing of the past, apart, that is, from a few writers who doggedly persevered in the old (and easier) way. The lead given by Vinnicombe and Maggs was eagerly followed by numerous researchers who published a series of papers giving the results of quantitative work in various regions. Vinnicombe's book *People of the Eland* and Harald Pager's *Ndedema* stand out as monumental numerical studies. The labour invested in this work was enormous. Rock art research had crossed its Rubicon.

But, even as the statistical movement gained momentum, some researchers began to feel that numbers were not the whole answer. Having counted all the eland, all the human figures and so on, they still did not know what the numbers *meant*. To return to our analogy with *The Last Supper*, they knew exactly how many people were seated at the table, but they did not know who they were, why they were there or what was happening. It soon became clear that, to get at the significance of southern African rock art, one had to go beyond numbers to their underlying meaning. The only way to discover their meaning was through genuine

San people sitting around a fire in the Kalahari in the 1950s (Photograph: Lorna Marshall).

San beliefs, not through simply looking at the depictions or counting them. It was then that researchers began to return to the San themselves.

During the 1950s and 1960s the work of Philip Tobias, the Marshall family and others had begun to focus attention on the Kalahari San. They were recognised as being among the last survivors of the hunter-gatherer way of life that humankind had followed for millennia. In 1957 Lorna Marshall published a paper on the San belief known as *n!ow*. This and her subsequent papers on San religion and the medicine dance, together with her daughter's touching book *The Harmless People*, were to have a profound influence on rock art research.

Thus it was that the two trends of the 1960s – statistical techniques and an interest in the Kalahari San – came together. The silent numbers forced researchers to turn to the San for explanations. At the same time, people went back to the old, largely forgotten nineteenth-century collections made by Orpen and Bleek and found that the San of long ago had essentially the same belief system as the modern Kalahari San, though there were, of course, differences. The Orpen collection is comparatively short, but the Bleek collection comprises nearly 12 000 pages of verbatim accounts of daily life, folklore and myths. A whole new field of discovery suddenly opened up. From then on, ethnography (the recorded beliefs and life-ways of people living in, for the most part, small-scale societies) was of central importance in southern African rock art research.

Today it all sounds so easy and so obvious, but it was neither in the 1960s and 1970s. For one thing, the vast Bleek collection and the smaller Orpen collection are not easy to understand. As we shall see in the following chapters, the ethnography, like the art itself, is couched in San idioms and metaphors. Both the ethnography and the art have to be interpreted and 'translated' into language Westerners can understand. Only then can we discover the links between them.

Moreover, we must remember that the San ethnography, very considerable though it is, is not complete in the sense that the ethnographers comprehensively recorded every belief, every ritual and every practice. Inevitably, there were things that Bleek and Lloyd and the more recent anthropologists never saw and things that the San did not think to tell them. Indeed, people seldom articulate their most fundamental values. We are thus working with an incomplete jigsaw puzzle, and, to make matters worse, we don't know how many pieces are missing. Often pieces we think are missing are in fact there: we just don't

know enough about San thought to
recognise them. Still, now that we
have rediscovered the San, we are
finding that the principal beliefs that
lie behind the art have been almost
miraculously preserved. Despite
difficulties with the way in which the
ethnography is phrased and despite the
limitations of what has been recorded,
we can form some idea of what the art
meant to those who made it and those
who looked at it.

Two Kalahari San women in the 1950s
(Photograph: Lorna Marshall).

THE KHOISAN LANGUAGES

The many San languages are all members of the Khoisan linguistic family, which comprises the languages spoken by the Khoekhoe (Hottentots) and the San (Bushmen). The best-known Khoekhoe language is Nama; today it is spoken by some 150 000 people. San linguistic groups such as the northern Kalahari !Kung, the central Kalahari G/wi and !Kõ, and the now-extinct southern /Xam have become familiar to students of the Khoisan through the writings of numerous anthropologists. Tony Traill describes the complex and not fully understood relationships between all these languages in
The Bushmen, edited by Philip Tobias (see Further Reading). He explains that, phonetically, they are the world's most complex languages. For Westerners, the most curious and distinctive sounds are the clicks. These sounds also occur in some Bantu languages, notably Zulu and Xhosa, where the clicks are represented by *c*, *q* and *x*, but they were borrowed from Hottentot and Bushman languages. The following descriptions of the four principal clicks – there are six all told – are based on Lorna Marshall's account

in *The !Kung of Nyae Nyae*.

• / or *Dental click*. The tip of the tongue is placed against the back of the upper front teeth; in the release, it is pulled away with a fricative sound. English-speakers use a similar sound in gentle reproof.

• ! or *Alveolar-palatal click*. The tip of the tongue is pressed firmly against the back of the alveolar ridge where it meets the hard palate and is very sharply snapped down on release. A loud pop results. English-speakers sometimes use the sound repeatedly to imitate the galloping of horses.

• ≠ or *Alveolar click*. The front part of the tongue, more than the tip, is pressed against the alveolar ridge and drawn sharply downward when released. Some English-speakers use something like this sound to express sympathy.

• // or *Lateral click*. The tongue is placed as for the alveolar click. It is released at the sides by being drawn in from the teeth. Drivers of horses sometimes use lateral clicks to signal their horses to start or to go faster.

Another sound which appears frequently is X. It is a gutteral sound as in the Scottish *loch*.

5

The interpretative approach: San beliefs

Recent research has shown that the trance dance and the spiritual experiences of shamans lie at the heart of San rock art. As we shall see in Chapter 9, there are many levels of meaning in the art, but it seems that its actual production was intimately bound up with this, the San's most important religious ritual. It even seems likely that most, possibly all, of the artists were themselves shamans who painted and engraved trance visions of the spirit world and symbols of the supernatural potency that enabled them to achieve their transcendent states. This is not to say that they painted and engraved while they were actually in trance. They tremble too much and, indeed, are often deeply unconscious. It seems more likely that they made their pictures after they had, as it were, returned to this world and could more serenely contemplate their tumultuous hallucinations. Because this shamanistic explanation is so deeply rooted in San thought, it has become generally accepted among archaeologists and anthropologists who are familiar with the art and with the San as the fundamental source of the art, whatever other meanings we may discern in it. We shall doubtless have to change our minds about details and aspects of this interpretation as we continue to unravel the highly complex and nuanced symbols, metaphors and implications of San shamanism, but the debate about the general framework of the art appears to be over.

To show how San beliefs about shamans and the spirit world explain the art we return to the 'mermaid' painting that baffled Sir James Alexander. It is illustrated here by means of a tracing Thomas Dowson made in 1988, or 153 years after Alexander saw it. This new tracing shows features that Major Michell, Alexander's guide, did not notice or did not consider worth recording in detail. As we shall see, these details are highly significant.

In 1878, three years after Wilhelm Bleek's death, Lucy Lloyd achieved a breakthrough when she showed

A copy made by T. A. Dowson in 1988 of a southern Cape rock painting. Compare this copy with C. C. Michell's 1835 copy on page 8.

//Kabbo, who taught Wilhelm Bleek and Lucy Lloyd much about the Cape San (Bleek and Lloyd Collection, University of Cape Town).

another but also incomplete copy of this painting to /Han≠kass'o, a man with a very interesting history. He was the son-in-law of //Kabbo, a fine informant who lived with the Bleeks in Cape Town from February 1871 to October 1873, when he travelled back to his home near Kenhardt. //Kabbo intended to return to Cape Town but died before he could do so. Efforts to obtain the services of other members of //Kabbo's family at first failed; finally Lloyd managed to arrange for /Han≠kass'o to come to Cape Town. Sadly, his wife died on the journey, despite the assistance given by the civil commissioner at Beaufort West. /Han≠kass'o seems to have had direct access to San traditions antedating the arrival of the first colonists because Lloyd noted that his father, Ssounni, 'died before the Boers were in that part of the country'. Like //Kabbo, /Han≠kass'o was, as Lloyd put it, 'an excellent narrator of Bushman lore, and a thoroughly efficient helper'.

The places where he and //Kabbo lived appear on a very rough sketch map that Bleek compiled from information they gave him. Bleek himself was not able to visit the area, and he had to suggest the scale of the map by using such phrases as '6 or 9 hours', 'a whole day's journey' and '15 days (a sheep path)'. Recently, Janette Deacon managed to decipher this sketch map and thus identify the actual places where /Han≠kass'o and //Kabbo lived. When she studied the rock engravings she found there, she discovered that the principal themes of the art relate to the activities and experiences of shamans rather than to the many myths that the San people recounted to Bleek and Lloyd.

It is, moreover, important to remember that /Han≠kass'o was familiar with rock paintings as well as engravings and told Lloyd a story in which he mentioned haematite and specularite as substances used in red and black paint respectively. He therefore had some first-hand experience with rock art, but he nevertheless admitted that he could not explain all the features of the 'mermaid' painting. The art in the region from which he came is much less complex than that in other parts of southern Africa, so it is to be expected that he would be puzzled by some of the details. It is more important to note his *general* interpretation and the context in which he understood the painting.

When /Han≠kass'o saw the 'mermaid' painting, he at once identified the figures as shamans of the rain who were protecting people from, curiously, 'the rain's navel' that was threatening to kill them. In other words, he saw the painting as in some way associated with the shamans' work. His puzzling phrase 'the rain's navel' is one of a set of anatomical metaphors: the San conceived of the rain as an animal of indeterminate species and spoke of its legs, hair, tail, blood and milk. When they wished to make rain, the shamans of the rain went into the spirit world of trance where they captured a hallucinatory rain animal or 'rain-cow', led it across the veld and then killed it so that its blood and milk would fall as rain. Dia!kwain, another of Lloyd's informants, told her that, when people are trying to chase away a dangerous thunderstorm – a 'rain-bull' – they 'strike their navels with their fists, and they press their hand in their navel and they snap their fingers at the rain'. We know that finger-snapping was a way of shooting supernatural potency at a person and

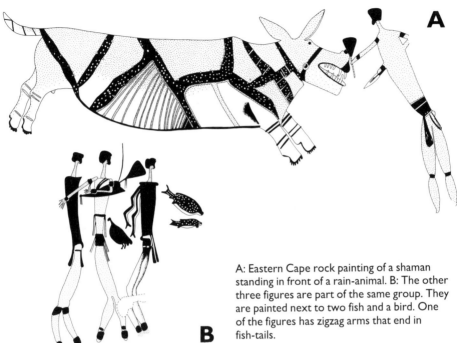

A

B

A: Eastern Cape rock painting of a shaman standing in front of a rain-animal. B: The other three figures are part of the same group. They are painted next to two fish and a bird. One of the figures has zigzag arms that end in fish-tails.

that potency was also situated in a shaman's stomach. Even though we cannot yet fully understand the phrase 'the rain's navel', /Han≠kass'o seems to have been talking about the danger of the thunderstorm's supernatural power and the way in which shamans shot their own power at the rain and thus protected people.

When /Han≠kass'o came to comment on the 'mermaid' figures, he said, 'I think they are the rain's people.' By 'rain's people' he meant those shamans who specialised in rain-making and protecting people from thunderstorms. He went on to say, 'They have their arms; they resemble people.' A few years ago our

knowledge of the art made it seem as if he was not particularly concerned about the 'fish-tails' and that he was saying that, whatever their legs looked like, they had arms and were therefore people. This is no doubt partly true, but there may be more to his explanation.

To understand better what he meant we turn to a painting of shamans (one of whom bleeds from the nose) and a rain-animal in which there is a feature that points to an important San concept: the shamans are painted next to two fish, and the arms of one of them end in fish-tails. The explanation for this is to be found in a San metaphor. Trance is like being under water because both conditions involve a sense of weightlessness, affected vision, difficulty in breathing, sounds in the ears, and eventual unconsciousness. The artists therefore used fish and sometimes eels to suggest the 'under-water' experience of trance. /Han≠kass'o may not have been puzzled by the fish-tails at all: he may have seen the figures as rain-making shamans partially transformed into fish in their 'under-water' experience.

A southern Cape rock painting of a 'swallow-shaman'.

More recent research suggests that the painting may in fact be better explained by another and in some ways complementary San metaphor. Perhaps because Sir James Alexander set our minds running along amphibious lines, most researchers have accepted the strange forms as fish-tails and so obscured what we now consider the better inter-pretation: the figures can be seen as having swallow-tails. This interpretation was first suggested by Joyce van der Riet and Dorothea Bleek. Then other paintings were found in the area that depict figures with similar tails and with long wing-like arms curving back parallel to their sides. One of these has a conventionalised human head with what appear to be the two antelope ears of a shaman-of-the-game's cap.

Flight is, of course, a worldwide metaphor for trance that arises from sensations of floating, dissociation from one's body, journeys to distant places and changes in perspective that include looking down on one's surroundings. That the San themselves thought of trance in terms of flight is clear from the ethnography. Dia!kwain told Lucy Lloyd that San shamans could turn themselves into birds; sometimes, he said, a bird-shaman would alight on a person's head. This statement recalls a painting showing a bird standing on a man's head.

Dia!kwain did not name a specific species of bird, but it is of interest that in another statement he said that the swallow was 'the rain's thing'. The word he used for swallow was *!kwerri-/nan*. The second part of this word is obscure, but the first part means to thunder or to strike (*!kwerriten*). Another /Xam word for swallow was /kabbi-ta-/khwa. Here it is the first part of the word that is obscure, but /khwa is another form of !khwa, rain; ta is a possessive. Thus whatever /kabbi and /nan may have meant, both words link swallows with rain. As one man put it, 'The swallows come when the rain clouds are in the sky.' We are beginning to see just how subtle and complex San thought is.

But the association goes even deeper. People were warned not to throw stones at swallows because 'the swallow is with the things which the sorcerers take out, which they send about. Those are the things which the swallow resembles.' /Ki, the word Lloyd translated 'take out', also means 'to possess' and was used to denote the control that shamans exercised over animals, potency and other things. A shaman could send one of the things he 'possessed', say, a butterfly, into a person and so make that person ill. We can now see that a swallow was another of the 'things' a shaman could possess. Dia!kwain expanded this idea when he told Lloyd that a certain man who did not heed the warning not to throw stones at swallows fell unconscious because 'the swallow had entered into him.' Dia!kwain then said, quite explicitly, 'A sorcerer had come out of the swallow into him.' For the San, a swallow could be the

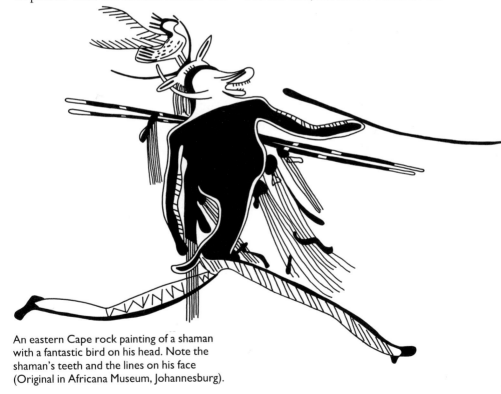

An eastern Cape rock painting of a shaman with a fantastic bird on his head. Note the shaman's teeth and the lines on his face (Original in Africana Museum, Johannesburg).

embodiment of a shaman.

These beliefs are particularly significant because, in the art, human beings are blended with other creatures as well as fish and birds. The most common examples show people with antelope heads and hoofs; others have elephant, baboon and bird-like features. The old, exclusively narrative approach to the art took these paintings and engravings literally as people wearing masks, costumes or hunting disguises. Today we know that therianthropes, as they are called, represent people blended with animal potency who are experiencing trance. When Lloyd showed Dia!kwain Orpen's copy of a painting of men with eland heads, he identified the figures as shamans 'who have things whose bodies they own'. These 'things', their animal personae or spirit helpers, enabled them to 'see' what ordinary people could not see.

In addition to blending with animals, people in trance experience other transformations as well. One of these results from the physical sensation of elongation and rising up that is sometimes experienced in trance. For instance, a Kalahari San shaman pointed to a tree and said he was that tall when he was in trance. Human figures are often painted or engraved in an elongated fashion, and this has given rise to the mistaken belief that the artists were depicting a mysterious tall race, that they were just trying to make themselves appear important, or that this was simply a stylistic feature. They were actually depicting a physical sensation, and that is probably the explanation for the greatly attenuated curved figure in the 'mermaid', or as we should probably now call it, the 'swallow-shaman' painting (p. 45). The painting that so baffled Alexander probably depicts shamans of the rain in their swallow

An Orange Free State rock painting of an elongated shaman with an antelope head.

personae surrounding a greatly elongated shaman.

Still other ways of talking about and depicting trance can be seen in an explanation J. M. Orpen obtained from Qing when they were looking at another rain-shaman painting in the Maluti Mountains. Qing's explanation is of the utmost significance to rock art research not just because he explained a puzzling painting but because he expressed a number of San ideas that can be used to explain a great many other paintings. The painting shows four people leading a rain-animal by means of a thong attached to its nose, while another two people confront a second rain-animal (p.53).

Qing began by declaring the animal to be a snake, at which point Orpen understandably inserted a parenthetical exclamation mark in his account of the interview. The apparent misidentification can, however, be explained. When Wilhelm Bleek showed the same painting to his informants, they identified it not as a snake but – more reasonably – as a rain-animal. Why, then, did Qing say 'snake'? In San thought, snakes are closely associated with rain and water; like swallows, they are said to be 'the rain's things'. There is also a widespread and perhaps related belief among Bantu-speakers about a large serpent that lives in deep pools. If we bear in mind that Qing's

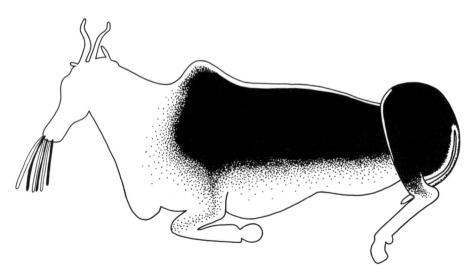

An eastern Cape rock painting of a dying eland with foam and blood falling from its mouth. Dying eland release their supernatural potency.

San concepts were being translated into a Bantu language before they were put into English, we should not be too surprised that the animal ended up as a snake.

Qing then went on to speak about the people who were capturing the animal:

1. They are holding out charms to it,
2. and catching it with a long riem (thong).
3. They are all under water,
4. and those strokes are things growing under water.
5. They are people spoilt by the (Moqoma) dance,
6. because their noses bleed.
7. Cagn gave us the song of this dance,
8. and told us to dance it,
9. and people would die from it,
10. and he would give charms to raise them again.
11. It is a circular dance of men and women,
12. following each other,
13. and it is danced all night.
14. Some fall down;
15. some become as if mad and sick;
16. blood runs from the noses of others
17. whose charms are weak.

[Lineation and **numbers added**]

All this was rather bewildering for Orpen, but today, thanks to Bleek's work and the recent research done with the Kalahari San, we know that Qing was describing the trance dance. In fact his description (lines 11-17) is very similar to the one Arbousset and Daumas gave nearly thirty years before (p. 29). Both accounts described the frenzy and, most important, the nasal blood, which shows they were both talking about, specifically, the trance dance.

The earlier missionaries added that Cagn, or '/Kaggen' as Bleek wrote the name, was 'worshipped' during the dance, and Qing said that Cagn had given them the 'song' of the dance (line 7). As we have seen, the 'song' of a dance contains its potency. This potency is also implied by the 'charms' (lines 10 and 17) that help to bring shamans back from the spirit world. It is possible that some of these 'charms' were aromatic herbs known as *buchu*. In San belief, potency can be conveyed or transmitted by strong scents.

Throughout his complex explanation Qing was using a series of three metaphors, or idioms. This is the real clue to understanding San rock art because the shaman-artists painted and engraved the same metaphors. The first of these metaphors is the one we have already discussed – under water (lines 3 and 4). According to Qing the capture of a rain-animal took place 'under water'. He developed this aquatic metaphor by declaring a scatter of short strokes (not shown in Orpen's published copy) to be 'things growing under the water' (line 4). When, nearly a century later, a modern Kalahari San shaman used the same metaphor in an account he gave to Megan Biesele, he said that a giraffe (the power animal of his trance dance) and God took him to a wide body of water: 'Then I entered the stream and began to move forward.' Secondly, Qing used a complementary metaphor, 'spoilt' (line 5). Megan Biesele has explained that the San word for 'to be spoilt' is still used in the northern Kalahari to mean to enter deep trance. Later in his statement Qing used a third metaphor for trance, 'death' (line 9), which is likewise still used in the Kalahari. It requires more explanation.

When he said that Cagn had told the people they would 'die' from the dance (line 9), he meant they would enter the spirit world just as people do when they die physically. This idea is expressed in the art through animal behaviour. The San saw parallels between the behaviour of a dying antelope, especially an eland, and a shaman 'dying' in trance. Both tremble, sweat profusely, stagger, bleed from the nose, lower their heads and eventually fall unconscious. An antelope's hair also stands on end, and the San believed hair grew on a man in trance. In the art, shamans are often shown bleeding, staggering, lowering their heads, and with hair standing on end. Sometimes they are placed next to dying eland because an antelope is believed to release its potency when it

J. M. Orpen's copy of a Lesotho rock painting depicting shamans catching rain-animals (1873) (South African Library, Cape Town).

dies. In the Kalahari today San hunters like to perform a trance dance next to a dead eland because they believe they can exploit its potency for a particularly effective dance.

Qing's rather involved explanation of the rain-animal painting shows that the San themselves recognised that the art should not be taken at face value: many of its features have deeper meanings that would escape us if we knew nothing about San beliefs. Once we have discovered these deeper meanings we have to go back and reconsider many of our ideas about what the art depicts. Fish, birds and the various ways of depicting death (e.g. p. 51), for example, should not be taken literally: they are metaphors expressing religious experience. Even the beautifully painted and engraved animals are not merely narrative depictions of what the San saw in the veld. We now know that they, especially eland, are symbols of potency and, as the therianthropes suggest, may sometimes be also shamans who have been completely transformed by their animal power. And then the depictions of hunting, whether explicitly shown by men chasing or shooting at animals or, more commonly, implied by their carrying quivers and hunting equipment, are showing events in the spirit world of trance (e.g. p. 23). A Kalahari shaman, for instance, explained that he had gone on an out-of-body journey during a trance dance and had killed an eland. The next day he and his family found the carcass and feasted. In real life as well as in the art the dividing line between this world and the spirit world is by no means clear.

After a dance, Kalahari shamans tell the people of trance experiences like this and everyone listens attentively to their revelations of the spirit world. San shamanism is not a secret religion. The art, too, was publicly displayed for all to see. The spirit world was actually in the midst of this world.

The supreme importance of the spirit world explains why key features like nasal bleeding, a hand raised to the nose, the arms—back posture, elongation, hair standing on end, bending forward, fish, birds and so forth often appear in apparently narrative scenes or associated with single human figures scattered through complex panels. They show the pervasive influence of trance experience in the art. Trance and the beliefs associated with it are the filter through which the real world passed before it appeared in the art. Some aspects of the real world were filtered out while those aspects that were, for one reason or another, important to the shaman-artists became prominent. Once we know about this filter, we are in a position to make discoveries, even in panels we have known for many years.

The interpretative approach:
Pictures in the brain

When researchers realised that San rock art was, at least essentially, shamanistic, they started to investigate neuropsychology, the branch of psychology that studies, amongst other things, the hallucinations people experience in altered states of consciousness. Most of the research that deals with hallucinations was conducted without any reference to shamanism or rock art and is therefore an independent source of evidence. It derives to a large extent from laboratory experiments using hallucinogenic drugs such as LSD. Rock art researchers hoped that neuropsychology would be able to answer such questions as: What sorts of visions do people in altered states of consciousness experience? Apart from visions, what other kinds of hallucinations do they experience? Do people's hallucinations have anything in common or are they all completely individual?

In answering these questions neuropsychological research has shown that, because the human nervous system is universal, all people who enter trance experience similar visual, auditory, physical and olfactory hallucinations, no matter what their cultural background. All the senses hallucinate. The different ways people interpret these hallucinations and the specific content of many visual hallucinations are, of course, controlled by the beliefs and experiences of a person's cultural background. Inuit (Eskimos), for instance, do not hallucinate eland; they 'see' polar bears.

Before we apply the results of neuropsychological research to San rock art, I must emphasise an important point of logic. We are not using neuropsychology to show that the art is the product of altered states of consciousness. As we saw in Chapter 5, we already know from the ethnography, and so quite independently of neuropsychology, that the art depicts the visions and experiences of shamans who entered trance. It is therefore reasonable to suppose that neuropsychological research can take us further by clarifying some aspects of depictions of those experiences on which the ethnography does not touch.

One of the most important components of neuropsychological research has in fact helped to explain the 'crosses, circles, points and lines … placed in a long rank' that so puzzled Sir John Barrow. These and other geometric forms, such as zigzags and nested U-shapes, are prominent at certain rock engraving sites, but they are also present, though less obviously so, in the paintings. In the first stage of trance all people, regardless of their cultural background, 'see' luminous zigzags, grids, vortices, sets of lines, meandering lines, dots and other geometric forms. These entoptic

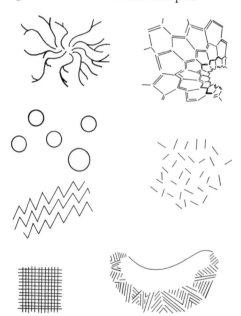

Some of the geometric entoptic phenomena seen by people in an early stage of trance.

phenomena, or entoptics as they are sometimes called ('entoptic' means within the optic system), can be seen with the eyes open or closed; if the eyes are open, the forms are projected onto surfaces such as walls or ceilings. They also expand and contract, fragment and combine. They can be induced by a wide variety of techniques. Taking hallucinogens is the most obvious way of entering trance and seeing entoptic phenomena, but they are also induced by rhythmic dancing and music, sensory deprivation, hyperventilation, prolonged and intense concentration, and, as many people know from experience, by migraine. To understand why they are less numerous among the paintings than among the engravings we must move on to the second stage of trance experience.

In this stage people try to make sense of the entoptic phenomena they are seeing. They elaborate the forms into objects important to them. This is where cultural background begins to play a role, because people tend to turn entoptic phenomena into things they have been brought up to associate with religious experience or into things related to the mood in which they happen to be. An example of this process of making sense is the U-shaped entoptic. It has a curved, flickering outside edge around a boat-shaped area of invisibility. The area of invisibility is a sort of 'black hole' which blots out anything in the 'real' world that it happens to cover. Some artists painted fairly literal depictions of this entoptic but with antelope legs and part-human, part-animal figures coming out of the area of invisibility (p. 61). One of these paintings even has zigzags to represent the flickering perimeter. Another very detailed painting has antelope heads on one side and human legs on the other. It gives the impression that the area of invisibility was, for this artist, an area of transformation where people and animals were joined in the spirit world. Other artists elaborated the U-shape into honeycombs. This is how wild honeycombs are shaped, and honey was, and in the Kalahari still is, closely associated with supernatural potency. Some of these paintings have bees with their wings carefully and minutely painted. All these curious paintings show how individual San shamans struggled to make sense of the luminous shapes which their nervous systems caused them to see as they went into trance.

As people move on from the second to the third and deepest stage of trance, they begin to lose their grip on reality. In this stage entoptic phenomena are less important, and people hallucinate animals, monsters and other things with a powerful emotional content. Instead of saying their visions are *like*, say, snakes, they say they *are* snakes. They themselves are also drawn into their visions and become, as it were, part of their own hallucinations. This is the experience that shamans interpret as a journey to the spirit world.

One of the interesting features of the third stage is that images are combined. For example, an animal may be combined with an entoptic phenomenon, or a person may be combined with an animal. A Westerner experimenting with a hallucinogen said that, in trance, he thought of a fox and was instantly transformed into a fox; he could see his long ears and bushy tail. It was this sort of experience that led San shamans to feel that they had turned into animals, to 'see' other people as half-animal, and then paint therianthropes – human beings fused with animals (pp. 50, 72, 73). Other features, such as blood falling from the nose, show that these combination paintings arose from shamanistic trance experience.

An understanding of these three stages has bearing on the question why there are more geometric forms among the rock engravings than among the paintings. For reasons that are not yet clear, it seems that some engravers tended to concentrate more on the first stage of trance than the painters did. Perhaps the engravers were concerned more – but by no

Rock engravings of entoptic phenomena (Photographs: T. A. Dowson).

A

B

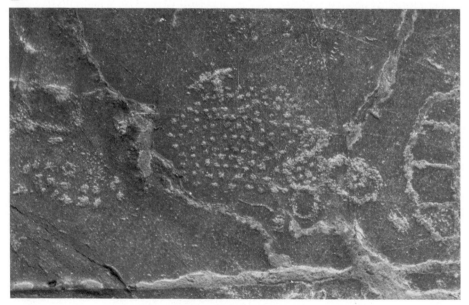

C

means entirely – with the initial acquisition of supernatural power and so with the entoptics of stage one, while the painters were concerned more with the experiences of deeper trance and thus depicted animals, people, therianthropes, rain-animals and so forth.

Neuropsychology also helps us to attempt an explanation of some features of the 'swallow-shaman' painting Sir James Alexander found so enigmatic (p. 8). In the first place, an undulating line in the upper right part of the painting appears in the copy Major Michell made for Alexander but not in the one that was given to Bleek. The most recent copy of the painting (p. 45) shows that there are in fact three wavy lines and some dots. The reason for the omission of these features is that when most people copy rock paintings they tend to copy only those parts they feel they can understand. Because we now have a much better understanding than any of the early copyists and because we know that the painting is associated with shamans of the rain and their trance experiences, we can suggest that the wavy lines depict an entoptic form. The fact that the lines are closely associated with the swallow-shamans suggests that this is a painting of a stage three hallucination.

Moreover, the curved form of the very attenuated figure and the way in which the smaller figures are placed along the outside of the curve strongly recall the boat-shaped entoptic phenomenon with its flickering perimeter (p. 61). As we have seen, it seems that some shaman-artists interpreted the flickering as the flashing legs of galloping antelope. In the case of Alexander's puzzling painting there are two other possible interpretations. Either a shaman-artist interpreted the flickering as a series of 'under-water' figures perhaps shimmering in the refraction of the surface of the water, or he associated the flickering with the erratic flight of swallows and the way in which they flash their wings open and closed as they swoop rapidly and change direction. Either way, the five central figures have been placed in the area of invisibility. A painting we have already discussed suggests that a Drakensberg painter took this area to be a place where people are transformed into antelope (p.61); this painter, living in the southern Cape coastal area, also thought in terms of transformation, but into fish or birds rather than antelope. Indeed, comparison of this painting with the Drakensberg one suggests that the same concept – transformation into other creatures – was associated with the boat-shaped entoptic phenomenon and its 'black hole' over a wide area of southern Africa and that individual shaman-artists depicted the experience of transformation into other creatures in different ways.

Moreover, the different ways in which individuals interpret their entoptic visions explain an apparent contradiction between the two explanations of J. M. Orpen's copy of the rain-animal scene (p. 53). Qing said that the 'strokes' scattered amongst the rain-shamans and the rain-animals were 'things growing under water', but Wilhelm Bleek's informant said the strokes indicated rain. We know from neuro-psychological research that one entoptic form is a scatter of flickering flecks that may be superimposed on normal vision or on other hallucinations (p. 56). Neuro-psychological research has also shown that, although people interpret their entoptic visions in different ways, these ways are none the less all within the limits of the general beliefs of their society. It seems likely that the shamans in the area from which Qing came interpreted the entoptic flecks scattered across their field of vision as 'things growing under water'. Thomas Dowson has argued that, because Qing did not use the word 'plants', it is possible that the 'things' are actually some manifestation of the potency which, so San shamans say, can be seen by people in trance, and that 'growing' refers to the way entoptic phenomena enlarge, flicker and move. On the other hand, the shamans living in the area from which Bleek's informant came saw their entoptic flecks as rain or water (they had only one word for water and rain). Rain, especially newly fallen rain, was also believed to have potency, and that, together with the fact that the shamans were protecting people from a thunderstorm, is why he identified the strokes as rain. The two explanations are thus not contradictory. They merely give two related interpretations of a universally experienced entoptic phenomenon, just as neuropsychological research leads us to expect.

By combining neuropsychological research with San beliefs we are able to approach southern African rock art from two separate but complementary perspectives. Neuropsychology tells us about the generation of mental imagery – why it takes the forms it does – and the ethnography tells us what these images meant to the San.

It would be wrong to suppose that researchers who draw on neuro-psychology are reducing all rock art to universal and therefore virtually meaningless physical reactions. The first part of 'neuropsychology' refers to the responses of the nervous system, but the second part (psychology) indicates that those responses must always be understood in terms of the particular culture in which they are experienced. Shamans are not unthinking photocopying machines churning out facsimiles of their hallucinatory experiences. Rather, they are active 'processers' of their experiences. Always, it is culture that is paramount, and, as I have argued, no art can be understood apart from its specific social and cultural setting.

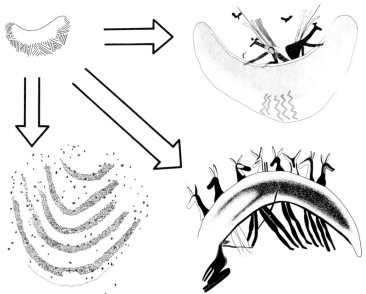

Three rock paintings probably derived from the entoptic phenomenon in the upper left corner.

7

Ducks and rabbits

Once we have appreciated the way in which San beliefs and neuro-psychological research complement each other in giving a better understanding of southern African rock art, we can go back and take a second look at many paintings and engravings the meanings of which have long been considered un-problematic. Just as a knowledge of Christianity helps us to see that the thirteen men seated at the table in Leonardo's *The Last Supper* are not *all* ordinary people – one of them, despite the fact that he has no 'supernatural' features, is supposed to be God made man – so, too, can we see that many apparently narrative 'scenes' in San art are far more complex than has been supposed. As with the optical illusion, narrative 'ducks' turn into symbolic 'rabbits'.

To show how even some very convincing examples of apparently narrative San rock art are something altogether different, we shall examine

A Drakensberg rock painting that has been interpreted as men crossing a rope bridge. Important features of the painting challenge this interpretation.

a well-known painting from the Natal Drakensberg, which, as far as I am aware, has been universally seen as evidence for the construction of bridges. One writer spun the following story around this painting:

It has the appearance of a bridge being crossed by a lively group of hunters or warriors who approach from the right. Two young men and an older … man face them and two women appear to applaud their arrival. A possible explanation is that the group of hunters are Bushmen who are crossing a bridge to retrieve two of their womenfolk who have been carried off by Blacks who are all away except for two youths and two older men. One of the older men appears to be in an inebriated condition under the bridge!

In a less sensational interpretation another writer observed that the San used 'rope ladders' and that someone then had 'the bright idea' of stretching a ladder across a narrow gorge. The painting, he says, shows the ends of the 'bridge' attached to two stakes. In his view the shelter in which the painting is to be found can be seen as the ' "drawing office" for the Bushman engineer'. He concludes by saying of the men apparently crossing the 'bridge', 'It is to be feared that they are showing off to the applauding women on the left, and one has fallen off the bridge and lies on the ground.'

The first of these tales clearly derives from the colonial stereotype we discussed in Chapter 2. The San are presented as helpless in the face of persecution by blacks, who, if given the chance, will do likewise to whites. Both tales show how San rock art can be reduced to something trivial and to something at which we can laugh. One wonders what Wilhelm Bleek and Lucy Lloyd would have said about this levity at the expense of other people's deeply held beliefs.

In contrast to these narrative 'readings' of the painting, we shall use San beliefs and neuropsychology in our attempt to unravel its deeper meaning. Even if the San did construct rope bridges, this painting is better explained in another way.

In the first place, at least three of the men crossing the 'bridge' are bleeding from the nose. As we have seen (pp. 29, 32), this is strong evidence for supposing that the painting has something to do with trance performance rather than daily, secular activities. Then the women at the left and another figure down right are not 'applauding' the antics of the men crossing a bridge: they are clapping the rhythm of medicine songs. Finally, four of the running figures are carrying flywhisks, artefacts closely associated with the trance dance.

All these features are observable by anyone at a trance dance. A second category of features is hallucinatory or conceptual and 'observable' only by people in trance. For instance, when a shaman enters trance, his or her spirit is 'seen' to leave the body through a 'hole' in the top of the head. One of the bleeding figures on the 'bridge' has two long lines emanating from his head, as do trance figures in many other paintings (p.33). These lines probably depict the spirit leaving on an out-of-body journey.

Another visionary feature is depicted below the 'bridge', where there are at least four trance-buck. Although these 'winged buck' have been interpreted as spirits of the dead, the shamanistic explanation accounts for more of their features. For one thing, when shamans enter trance, they are believed sometimes to fuse with the animal potency they possess. A Kalahari shaman expressed this belief when he told Polly Wiessner that he saw himself as the antelope he had tried to kill when he first obtained potency.

Often trance-buck and therianthropes are shown with their arms in the backward position said to be associated with asking God for potency (p.65). Still other paintings have, in addition, 'streamers' emanating from the back of the neck or from between the shoulder blades, as do the trance-buck below the 'bridge'. These 'streamers' are occasionally difficult to distinguish from arms in the backward, trancing posture. It is from the nape of the neck that shamans expel the sickness they remove from their patients. Expelled sickness can be 'seen', so the shamans say, only by people in trance, and this fact, together with other considerations, suggests that trance-buck depict hallucinations of shamans transformed by potency.

The combination of observable features of the San trance dance (flywhisks, nasal bleeding, clapping women and the arms-back posture) and ethnographically verifiable San hallucinations (the spirit leaving the body and trance-buck) therefore clearly indicates that, whatever the 'bridge' may be, the painting has some connection with trance performance. Even if we could go no further, we should already have good reason to doubt the depiction of a bridge. Fortunately, we are now able to suggest a more credible interpretation.

This new explanation starts with the transformation of shamans in trance. When Richard Katz was working with the Kalahari San, he asked them to draw pictures of themselves. Those who had never experienced trance produced simple stick figures. The shamans, in contrast, drew zigzags and spirals which bear no resemblance to a human body. It seems that they were identifying themselves with the geometric entoptic phenomena that people see in altered states of consciousness. They *felt* a trembling in their bodies,

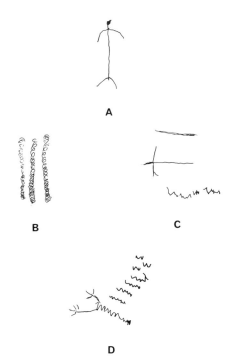

A

B   C

D

Drawings made for Richard Katz by Kalahari San. A: Drawing by a man who had never experienced trance. B, C and D: Drawings showing how San shamans conceive of themselves even when not in trance.

falling from its nose. The 'hairs' on this and other depictions are probably another kind of hallucination: people from various cultural backgrounds who have experienced trance report a tingling or prickling sensation on various parts of the body including the outsides of the arms. The Kalahari San speak of this prickling sensation along the spine, and Wilhelm Bleek's San people claimed that 'lion's hair' grew on the back of a shaman in trance – a feature that is sometimes painted. This suggests that some San interpreted the universally experienced tingling sensation as the growth of hair and associated transformation into an animal. In this instance the 'hairs' on the trance-buck's arms are clearly similar to the 'hairs' on the 'bridge'. Now note how the 'hairs' point away from the left- and from the right-hand ends of the 'bridge', even as the 'hairs' on the arms of the trance-buck point

and they *saw* shimmering zigzags. Then, in a process recognised by neuropsychology, they linked the physical sensations and the visual hallucinations: in the end, they *were* what they saw and felt.

This sort of experience is closely associated with other physical hallucinations. Some trance-buck have elongated, backward-extending arms covered with long 'hairs' One of these is on a large fallen boulder only a few metres from the 'bridge' painting. Like many trance-buck, it has blood

A Drakensberg rock painting of a transformed shaman with hairy 'arms' extended backwards; blood falls from his nose.

away from the body. Indeed, comparison of the arms of the hairy trance-buck with the two 'ropes' of the 'bridge' demonstrates beyond reasonable doubt that they are two expressions of the same idea. The 'bridge' is in fact two transformed shamans with their hirsute arms extended towards each other and merging.

Other aspects of the painting now snap into sharper focus. For instance, the elongation of the arms is probably another physical hallucination: as we have seen, people in trance often experience attenuation of their bodies and limbs, and many San paintings and engravings show this (p.50). Furthermore, comparisons of the heads of the 'pegs' with the heads of the first three human figures from the left and the recumbent figure below the 'bridge' to the right show that the tops of the 'pegs' are shaped like some painted human heads. In any event, the heads face in the wrong direction to function usefully as the heads of pegs securing a rope bridge. If we take all these points into consideration, the 'pegs' can be seen as bodies without legs and with heads facing inwards.

Such a radical alteration of the human body is, as Katz's San friends' drawings of zigzags and spirals showed, well within the bounds of San trance experience and, unlike a bridge, fits in with the other visual and physical hallucinations depicted in the painting. Indeed, this view unites the apparently diverse features of the painting in a single, coherent explanation that is rooted in San beliefs and neuropsychological research. Even the bows and arrows, which may be thought to be out of place in a trance situation, are compatible because men go hunting in the spirit world of trance experience.

A remaining problem is why seven of the human figures appear to be running on the extended arms of the 'trance-formed' shamans. In trying to explain this feature of the painting we must acknowledge, as we did when discussing the aesthetic approach, that we still know very little about San ideas of perspective and 'composition'. Their painted 'scenes' were probably composed according to conventions unknown in Western art. It is possible that no fixed or 'real' relationships, as understood by Westerners, are intended in many San rock art 'scenes': some of the apparent 'scenes' may actually portray figures individually and even at different times and therefore not capture an instant in the manner of a photograph. Many of the relationships that Westerners see in San rock art may be no more than optical illusions.

Though we are still far from a full understanding of the relationships depicted in the 'bridge' painting, it is worth noting that these are not the only depictions of people or animals

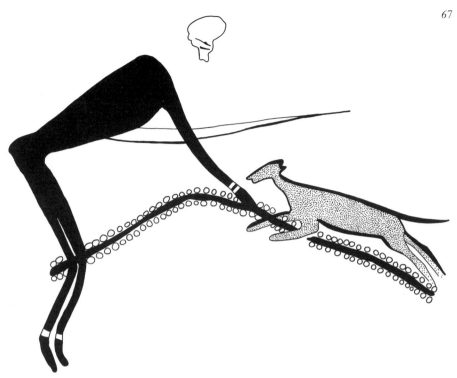

An eastern Cape rock painting of a man holding a red 'non-real' line with white dots while an animal appears to run along it.

apparently walking or running along lines. In some paintings the line is patently non-realistic in one part, where it may be shown entering or leaving the bodies of antelope, while another part may be held by a man as if it were a rope. It has been argued that many of these lines represent the potency activated and harnessed by shamans. If the zigzags drawn by Katz's friends can depict a human body, it is, as Thomas Dowson has argued, possible that some of the painted lines also depict shamans identifying themselves or others with potency.

A more specific interpretation of the relationship depicted in the 'bridge' painting may be that it expresses the San belief that shamans in trance pool their experience and protect one another with their potency: the more potency that is 'boiling' and being transmitted from one shaman to another, the more effective the trance. Shamans hold and embrace one another to transmit potency. The men apparently running on the hairy arms of the trance-formed shamans may, therefore, be deriving power from them, though not in any strict temporal or spatial sense. The real relationship is probably entirely conceptual, symbolic or hallucinatory, and the one suggested by Western perspective (running along a 'bridge') an illusion, but we have a long way to go before we can be more precise. Nevertheless, the painting clearly has more to do with the spirit world of trance experience than with the world of daily life.

Our examination of the 'bridge' has shown beyond reasonable doubt that San ethnography and neuro-psychology together explain far more about southern African rock art than the old way of looking at it and guessing what it depicts – let alone what it *means*. This work has only just begun. We are discovering more and more unsuspected details in painted panels and on engraved rocks, and these details are transforming our understanding of familiar depictions.

8

Battling it out

None of the discoveries that have deepened our understanding of San rock art has been achieved without a struggle and, sometimes, a good deal of bitterness. Right from the start, controversy and debate have been the order of the day. In retrospect, some of these debates are amusing, and we can now smile at all the extravagant claims. But at the same time we should try to look beneath the surface of the arguments and ask what was motivating the various writers. In some instances, it may have been personal glory. In other cases, there are deeper currents that have to do with the ways people perceive the San. These views can insidiously pervert a reader's understanding of the San.

A researcher who dominated rock art research for many decades was the French prehistorian, the Abbé Henri Breuil. He had achieved fame at the beginning of the twentieth century through his work on the Upper Palaeolithic cave art of France and Spain, and his forceful personality soon made him an authority on rock art worldwide. Between the two World Wars and then again during World War Two he came to southern Africa and made many pronouncements on the rock art here. Some of his views were resisted at the time, but they nevertheless had a lasting impact on people's ideas about the art, and some still live on in the popular imagination. One of his most celebrated blunders was his claim that a painting in the Brandberg, Namibia, depicted a woman of Mediterranean origin. Today people still speak of the White Lady of the Brandberg, even though the painting depicts a male and is an ordinary, if quite striking, San painting.

Towards the end of the 1940s Breuil made similar claims about certain paintings in the Natal Drakensberg. These paintings had been published as long ago as 1903 in the *Natal Railway Guide* and then in 1915 in *Scientific American* where they were accompanied by a short account of the San. In 1925, Raymond Dart, an enthusiastic proponent of the theory that Babylonian, Phrygian, Phoenician and Chinese clothing was depicted in southern African rock art, claimed these paintings revealed contact between the San and

Part of a complex Drakensberg rock painting panel formerly thought to depict Phoenicians.

Phoenicians. Unlike others, he did not claim that foreigners made the paintings, only that the San saw the various items of clothing and then painted them. Just over twenty years later Breuil visited the site and took up this interpretation. He described what he termed 'a robe or tunic of variable length, … a circular cloak' and sheepskin cloaks 'known to us

through the Sumerian works of art'. Similar figures painted in a long line were said to 'resemble those on the Babylonian and Persian monuments'. The great age of these paintings was supposed to be supported by what he called the 'fossil' nature of the rock on which they were painted. A child of his time, Breuil was seeing the world from a European perspective. In his view, European colonisation of the world in the seventeenth, eighteenth and nineteenth centuries had brought light to dark continents; he also believed that Europeans had similarly penetrated to remote and backward parts of the world in millennia long past, and this was shown by ancient rock art. In the more recent European expansion, history was merely repeating itself and emphasising the vast gap between Europeans and those whom they regarded as the 'primitive' people of other continents. European civilisation had advanced since Babylonian times, but elsewhere people had remained unchanged, incapable of improving themselves without European influence.

Not everyone accepted Breuil's claims. One of the sceptics was J. F. Schofield. In an article published in the *South African Archaeological Bulletin* in 1948, he rejected Breuil's inter-pretation and instead claimed that the cloaked figures were 'well-to-do Basuto women ... The real problem raised by these figures lies in the truly astonishing fact that similar figures dressed in a similar manner ... may be seen on any day of the week in the same neighbourhood.' He dismissed the ancient mariners and the mines they were supposed to be seeking as a myth. Schofield also wanted to know exactly what the Abbé meant by the word 'fossil' because he doubted the great antiquity that Breuil proposed

for the paintings. The editor seems to have been pleased with the paper and, in commending it to his readers, he said Schofield's 'considerable perspicuity' brought us back to 'a more orthodox view'.

The Abbé Breuil, on the other hand, was incensed. With elaborate irony he thanked Schofield for his 'perfect courtesy' and then bitterly went on to say that Schofield 'thinks to reduce to nothing ... the sum total of those conclusions and hypotheses that long contact with many groups of this art have led me to elaborate'. In response to Schofield's point that Bantu-speaking people could be observed wearing similar 'cloaks', Breuil argued that the Bantu-speakers 'have preserved right up to today costumes and customs that were far more ancient, and whose first appearance in this country was not their doing'. Schofield's view, he concluded rather smugly, 'is not mine nor that of other persons of distinction'. In response to Schofield's doubts about the 'fossil' nature of the rock, he again appealed to his experience rather than to any real evidence: 'I am enabled by my long experience of rock paintings in Spain to affirm absolutely the *fossil* age of a noteworthy proportion of those of Southern Africa.'

Needless to say, Schofield was not intimidated by all this bluster. In 1949 he came back with a paper modestly entitled 'Four Debatable Points'. One of his points was that research on the weathering of granite showed that the rate of decay made it unlikely that many of the paintings on it could be much older than a thousand years and thus could not depict Phoenicians and Babylonians. He went on to argue, this time in greater detail, that many of the items associated with the supposed foreigners, such as flywhisks and fringed karosses, were undoubtedly made by local Bantu-speaking farmers and could not be used as evidence for foreign influence.

More daringly, Schofield widened his criticism to include Professor C. van Riet Lowe of the South African Archaeological Survey who had recently caused a stir by identifying a Greek musical instrument, the aulos, in some Drakensberg paintings. Schofield insisted, apparently rightly, that the painted object did not in fact resemble the aulos. He also expressed regret that van Riet Lowe had brought in Egyptian mythology by referring to the antelope-headed figure holding the supposed aulos as 'Anubis-like'. Emphasising the futility of such far-fetched comparisons, Schofield wrote, 'Not only was Anubis a jackal but no figure should be described as being like him unless we know that it engendered in its authors similar emotions to those which he inspired in his own votaries.'

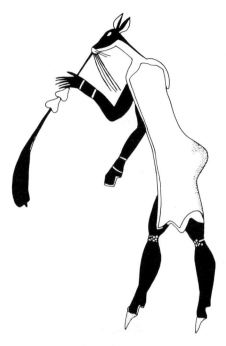

A Drakensberg rock painting of a therianthropic shaman. It has been claimed that this figure is holding an ancient Greek musical instrument, but this interpretation is no longer accepted.

This time the editor somewhat pusillanimously tried to avoid open conflict with the influential Abbé and the professor and so wrote only of 'uncertainty concerning recent discoveries in South African cave-paintings'.

As it turned out, Breuil and van Riet Lowe were wrong about the foreigners. Schofield and later writers who said that the cloaked figures were Bantu-speakers were also wrong – though perhaps less so. What is interesting in this debate is that no one seems to have examined the paintings carefully enough. The kaross-clad figures are not even human: they have hoofs instead of feet. The same is true of the figure holding the supposed aulos. All of them bleed from the nose. The supposed foreigners are therefore shamanistic therianthropes of the kind we have already discussed.

For some years the debate about the depiction of foreigners in San rock art

An eastern Cape rock painting of a buck-headed snake bleeding from the nose (Original in South African Museum, Cape Town).

A Drakensberg rock painting of a therianthropic shaman with hoofs.

seemed to be dead, but it was resurrected as recently as 1987 by a writer who went further than Dart, Breuil or van Riet Lowe by claiming that long ago people from Europe sailed up such rivers as the Zambezi, the Orange and, most incredibly, the Matjies, and then actually 'transmitted their beliefs and art to the Bushman hunters' who until that time had been ignorant of painting. In support of this astonishing suggestion the writer points to the buck-headed snakes of southern African rock art and claims that they depict ships with ornamental, carved prows. These ships, he says, were hauled overland when the rivers were too shallow. In fact, many of these buck-headed snakes bleed from the nose and are accompanied by people in trancing postures. There can be little doubt that they represent the San belief that shamans can travel underground as snakes do. But again the important point is that this writer, like so many of his predecessors, has not bothered to familiarise himself with San beliefs or to examine the art at all closely. The art has become a vehicle for Eurocentric views about the origins of art and civilisation.

This recent claim and the older arguments in favour of Phoenician painters all seem to be based on the assumption that nothing good can come out of Africa. Digging deeper, one may wonder what political and racial views the proponents of these theories hold. Are they really the disinterested scientists they claim to be or do they harbour deep-seated animosities and hidden political agendas? Even Great Zimbabwe, it will be recalled, was at one time said to have been built by people who came from beyond the shores of Africa. Indeed, a few years after the Unilateral Declaration of Independence in Rhodesia, as it then was, the white government insisted that a guidebook to Great Zimbabwe give equal space to the discredited view that the ruins had been in some way associated with foreign builders. This despite the fact that archae-ologists had shown that Great Zimbabwe was the centre of an extensive Shona state and that it was abandoned as recently as A.D. 1450. Using Shona beliefs and the reports of early Portuguese travellers, Thomas Huffman has been able to elucidate the symbolism of the way in which

Great Zimbabwe was laid out. But, despite all the research and evidence, the old beliefs about foreign influences persist.

As the recent book about ancient Europeans sailing up the Matjies River shows, this sort of thinking has not yet been eradicated from southern African rock art studies. While some researchers have worked hard to get at the truth about southern African rock art, others have preferred to preserve mystery and uncertainty. After all, many people find a mystery more exciting than an explanation.

Throughout all the debates the San themselves have been denigrated or, at best, overlooked. Even though today professional archaeologists and anthropologists accept that authentic San beliefs explain the art in great detail – certainly better than any foreign beliefs and influences – there is still a tendency for some researchers to speak as if they can plumb the meaning of the art simply by looking at it. In doing so they exalt Western achievements and denigrate the San.

9

Many meanings

So far we have concentrated on the shamanistic meanings of San rock paintings and engravings because it seems clear that the art arose out of the experiences of shamans. But just what we mean by 'meanings' is not as clear as it may seem. Philosophers debate – but cannot agree on – the meaning of 'meaning'. The word is rather like the rock art images themselves: both have many meanings. I am going to sidestep the philosophical debate and introduce some of the problems by referring again to *The Last Supper*.

One could easily say that, in one rather simple sense of the word, Leonardo's painting 'means' Christ's institution of the Eucharist. Perhaps there would not be much disagreement about that. But, when we come to look in detail at the ways in which the disciples are painted, we can see that various archetypal attitudes to Christ are suggested: Judas, the traitor, leans away from Christ; Philip rises from his seat and touches his breast as if to protest he is not the betrayer; Peter turns to speak to his neighbour, apparently ignoring Christ in a posture that foreshadows

his betrayal of the Lord. Then we can consider the painting from a different point of view: the private meanings it held for individuals. Now we find ourselves in an area of diverse and even contradictory meanings. For some of the monks in the monastery the picture probably evoked pleasant feelings about the supremacy of the Church and the eventual overthrow of those who, like Judas, oppose her. Perhaps, too, the painting was a kind of perpetual grace, blessing the food the monks ate and acknowledging that it was all God-given. On the other hand, the meanings the picture held for a poor peasant, especially one of a radical turn of mind, may have been quite different. Such a peasant may have resented the power of the Church and thought that the picture proclaimed a grossly unjust inequality. Apart from the fact that some monks worked in the fields, it was *he*, not God, who supplied food by his unremitting toil, and, to make matters worse, he was not paid a fair wage. At least part of the meaning of the painting thus derives from the viewer's attitudes and beliefs. Then it is worth pointing out that all the people seated at the table are men. Whether Leonardo intended it or not, the picture is making a statement about male domination of the Church hierarchy: it justifies the subordinate position of women in the Church. These few comments on the multiple meanings of *The Last Supper* show that we must probably allow that San people may also have seen their rock pictures in a variety of different ways and that the pictures had not just one simple meaning but many meanings.

In the early 1970s, when it became apparent to researchers that there was much more to the rock art than met the casual eye, they started to investigate the concept of polysemy —

that is, the multiple meanings that depictions can carry. They started by thinking especially about the range of meanings that can be conveyed by a symbol. For example, in Western society the cross can mean 'This is a grave', 'This is a church', 'This is a hospital', and then, beyond these simple meanings, it has associations of sacrifice, resurrection, compassion and so forth. Indeed, as anthropologists recognise, a symbol like the cross has the power to move people precisely because of its polysemy. If the cross could have such a range of meanings, rock art researchers wondered if the eland, the most frequently depicted animal in many parts of southern

An eastern Cape rock painting of an eland (Photograph: T. A. Dowson).

Africa, also had many meanings. If those meanings could be discovered, they would contribute greatly to our understanding of the art. When researchers turned to the ethnography, they found that the eland was indeed polysemic.

Some of the meanings the San attached to eland can be seen in their use of respect words for this animal. In certain circumstances, they felt the usual, everyday word to be too 'strong', and they avoided using it by employing a substitute word. In the different San languages, there are in fact two respect words, one for use by women and another for use by men. We shall examine the respect words that are part of the northern !Kung and the southern /Xam languages. In the northern Kalahari, San women avoid the usual word for eland, *!n* (simply a nasalised click), when they are performing the Eland Bull Dance, and instead say *dabba*. This dance is performed when a girl enters puberty. The men leave the camp, taking their hunting equipment with them. The girl is isolated in a small hut, and the women dance around it imitating the mating behaviour of eland cows. Then an old man, who has remained in the camp for this purpose, ties eland horns to his head and pretends to be an eland bull. As he approaches the women, they sway their hips thus causing the 'tails' of ostrich eggshell beads they are wearing to swing from side to side, just as the eland cows flick their tails when they are mating. The

Kalahari San women performing the Eland Bull Dance (Photograph: Lorna Marshall).

San consider this to be the climax of the dance, and the girl in the hut is so moved by the occasion that she weeps. This climax is reflected in the women's respect word for eland that the southern /Xam San used: ≠kouken-!khwi. Lloyd had some difficulty in translating this word, but in the end she found it means 'when it lashes its tail'. Clearly, it refers to the climax of the Eland Bull Dance.

But what are the associations of the Eland Bull Dance that so move the girl secluded in the hut? Asked about the benefits bestowed by the dance, an old San woman replied thoughtfully, with a distant look in her eyes,

They do the Eland Bull Dance so that she will be well; she will be beautiful; that she won't be thin; so that if there is hunger, she won't be very hungry and she won't be terribly thirsty, and she will be peaceful. That all will go well with the land and that rain will fall.

The meanings of the eland thus go far beyond the girl's puberty and fertility to include the well-being of all the people: everyone participates in the great event and receives the manifold blessings that derive from it. These blessings include even rain. The link between eland and rain can be clearly seen in a myth in which an eland is killed and its meat becomes rain, in the same way that a rain-animal is killed and becomes rain. The intensity of the Eland Bull Dance is so great and the meanings of the eland are so comprehensive that it is no wonder that the northern Kalahari San believe that an eland actually runs up to the dance; its appearance frightens the people, but the old man dancing the part of the eland bull reassures them that it is a 'good thing' which comes from God. The eland is the 'good thing' *par excellence*.

A San boy's entry into adulthood is not marked by such a dance. Instead, he is considered a man when he has killed his first large antelope, preferably an eland. He is then scarified with fat taken from parts of the eland that are considered to have potency. This is done while he is sitting on the eland's skin. Using a leg from the eland, one of the older men makes a circle of hoof prints around the skin. When the ritual is over, the boy drops his bow, plucking the string as he does so. As the San say, 'That is how eland will fall for him when he goes to hunt.' He then leaves the skin and crosses the circle of hoof prints: 'That is how he will find eland tracks in future.' Asked why they perform this ritual, a man replied, 'His heart is burning hot towards meat; he desires meat. He has become a real hunter and will spend the whole day out and not come back to camp.'

When out hunting, the southern San men avoided using their usual word for eland, *sa*, and substituted *ein*, meat. For all the San, northern and southern, meat is much more than food. The killing of an eland is an important social event because it brings together many people. As the meat is handed round and shared, it comes to symbolise social relationships and the unity of the people.

A number of ideas from both the Eland Bull Dance and the boys' first-kill rituals are summed up in San marriage rituals when the bride is anointed with eland fat. Fat is the essence of the eland and all that it means. A red design is also placed on her forehead and cheeks. Lorna Marshall could not find out what the red markings meant, but they may refer to the tuft of red hair on an eland's forehead and so recall the close association of a girl at puberty with the eland.

Different associations are evoked by the northern Kalahari men's respect word for eland, *tcheni*, which means 'dance'. It seems that this word does not refer especially to the Eland Bull Dance but rather to the medicine dance. The San consider the eland to have more supernatural potency than any other animal, and shamans like to 'dance eland power'. As they do so, they blend with the eland, a hallucinatory experience often depicted in the art. Then, as they begin to share their visions, they draw each other's attention to eland standing out in the darkness beyond the firelight, spirit eland but none the less real.

The respect words *dabba*, *≠kouken-!khwi*, *ein* and *tcheni* suggest just some of the eland's associations or 'meanings': clearly, the eland symbol reaches into many parts of San thought and ritual. A rock picture of an eland thus triggered more and very different meanings in the San mind than it does in a modern Western mind. One could go so far as to say that 'eland' is a hopelessly inadequate translation of *!n* or *sa*, the everyday San words for this antelope, because it leaves out most of the connotations of the San words. For English-speakers, 'eland' means little more than the largest African antelope, *Taurotragus oryx*; for the San, *!n* or *sa* and the various respect words opened a cornucopia of ideas.

But why *eland*? Why not some other animal? During a discussion of various antelope, a San man told me that female antelope have more fat than males. With the eland, however, the position is uniquely reversed: he pointed out that the male has more fat than the female. For the San, the eland is almost androgynous in that, by the male's possession of so much fat, the usual differentiation between the sexes is reversed.

This idea is expressed by a truly remarkable and, as far as we know, unique rock engraving of an eland that has two neck lines: one has a large, pendulous male dewlap; the other is a smaller female neck. It also

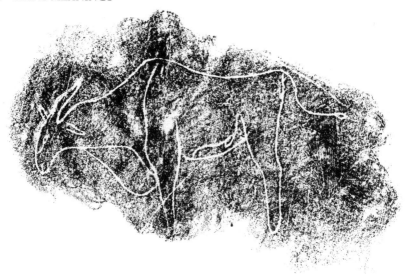

A Transvaal rock engraving of an eland with male and female neck and belly lines.

has a male belly line with a penis and a curving female belly line. Thomas Dowson, the discoverer of this engraving, argues that the rituals we have looked at in this chapter show that the San think of the eland as standing between a number of oppositions: male and female, availability and non-availability for marriage, this world and the spirit world. The shaman likewise bridges two worlds. As Dowson puts it, 'The engraving of the bisexual eland … represents one artist's insights into the anomalous status of both the eland and the shaman.' He also points out that mental images are combined in trance; just what those images are and what they mean depend on a person's cultural background. When these specifically San concepts were 'seen'

in a hallucination that combined images in a highly unusual way, something like this eland was the result. The shaman who experienced the hallucination then depicted it on the rock.

Another slant on the eland's sexual ambiguity has recently been suggested by John Parkington and Anne Solomon. In the mid–1960s Patricia Vinnicombe observed that 'The paintings … reflect a distinctly masculine bias', a conclusion to which Tim Maggs also came. Parkington and Solomon argue that this bias is an ideological statement that obscures the real economic relations between men and women: women in fact contribute more to San diet than do men. In the light of this ideology Solomon suggests that the eland is not just androgynous but that the painted eland are ultimately a statement about male domination in San gender relations. As with *The Last Supper*, San art justifies male domination.

The art in general has a range of what we can call 'economic' associations. Shamans who controlled the weather and the movements of antelope herds thereby controlled – or believed they could control – the production of food. Even those who simply cured sickness influenced food production indirectly. Hunters between whom there is some friction do not cooperate, and everyone in the camp suffers a meat shortage. The medicine dance can dissolve these tensions because, as Megan Biesele noticed, dancing in rhythmic unity tends to banish ill-feeling: San men who would not speak to each other before a dance can be seen chatting amicably after a dance. Moreover, a hunter who is suffering a run of bad luck will often request a shaman to 'cure' him and remove from him whatever it is that is spoiling his hunting. After such a ritual a hunter will go out into the veld with renewed confidence. Finally, shamans believe they go on out-of-body journeys to distant camps; on their return, they tell the people at home about what they believe is happening to their friends and relations. These sorts of far-flung ties are economically essential because in times of localised drought camps have to split up, and people go to live with others in better-watered areas.

These few comments show that shamanism has a lot to do with economic activity and with the good social relations within a camp and between camps that are vital for the short- and long-term survival of San society. Taken all in all, the art communicates these associations, not simply by depicting activities such as hunting, but, as a backdrop to daily life, it constantly reminded people of the sort of behaviour they valued and the importance of the shamans. More specifically, these ideas were summed up by the paintings and engravings of eland, the antelope which, above all others, made the shamans' beneficial activities possible through its extraordinary potency.

Patricia Vinnicombe expressed a similar idea when she argued that the San saw the form of their society reflected in the changing structure of eland herds. A number of small San camps amalgamate, usually in the spring when food is plentiful, and then split up into smaller units for the winter. In the Drakensberg, groups of eland similarly amalgamate in the spring when the new, sweet grass is coming up and then break up into smaller groups for the winter. In Vinnicombe's view, this pattern led to the eland becoming a symbol of San society. She summed it up like this:

'The eland was the pivot of a value structure around which the stability of the social organism was dependent.'

All these various meanings, or associations, of the eland are rather like parts of a spectrum: they are different and yet at the same time they grade into one another and are part of a single entity. When light is passed through a filter, parts of the spectrum may be excluded while other parts are highlighted. That is what rituals do to the spectrum of meanings possessed by a symbol. When the eland symbol – an actual eland or simply the eland concept – is used in ritual contexts, parts of its meanings are highlighted and other parts remain in the background, subdued but still contributing to its power. For example, when the concept of the eland is evoked in the Eland Bull Dance by the women's and the old man's dancing, it is the ideas of fatness, well-being and rain that are emphasised. In the boys' first-kill rituals, on the other hand, the prominent ideas are meat and all the social relationships implied by meat.

But what about the art? Do *all* the meanings of the eland resonate equally or, as in other ritual contexts, are certain meanings highlighted? As we have seen, very numerous features of the art together with what little ethnographic information we have on its production point to the depictions being primarily associated with

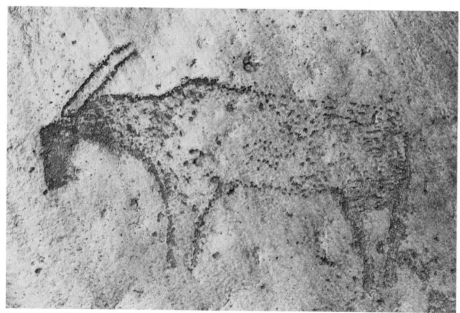

A northern Cape rock engraving of an eland. (**Photograph:** T. A. Dowson)

shamanistic beliefs and rituals. It therefore seems likely that the eland's power to bridge worlds and its trance associations were in the foreground and that the other meanings were in the background. It is easy to imagine a shaman consciously using rock art to make a statement about his experiences in the spirit world; it is less easy to imagine people *consciously* producing all that art to make a statement about, say, the ideology of gender relationships. That sort of meaning was there but in the background and in all probability not consciously depicted. Similarly, a painting of a trance dance makes its first and foremost statement about shamanism, even though the depictions of dancing men and clapping women come trailing their own clouds of additional associations such as gender relationships or the need for cooperation in hunting.

In this chapter I have concentrated on the eland, but the concept of polysemy can be extended to all the other kinds of depiction; there is simply not the space to explore *all* the resonances of the art. In any event, we still have a lot to learn about those resonances. But at least we can see that the meaning of San rock art cannot be reduced to a simple, straightforward statement, any more than the varied and subtle meanings of *The Last Supper* can be reduced to a simple statement like 'Christ instituting the Eucharist'. Since rock art researchers realised this some years ago, they have been following up various meanings. As they proceed, they find that, even though shamanism permeates all aspects of San thought and life and even though the art originated in shamanism, the field opens up before them: it does not narrow down. San rock art is a monument to the breadth, subtlety and interrelatedness of San thought.

10

The broken string

As our work of discovery continues, we must not lose sight of the *people* whose beliefs and art we are getting to know. Followers of all three approaches – aesthetic, narrative and interpretative – usually present the artists themselves in only the vaguest and most generalised way, perhaps as 'hunters' or 'primitives', never as people with hopes and fears, insights and passionately held beliefs.

By contrast, some of the most recent rock art research has tried to reinstate the individuals who made the art. Thomas Dowson, for instance, has gone beyond trying to trace the 'style' of specific artists to isolating the contributions individual shaman-artists made to religious knowledge. As Megan Biesele found, the Kalahari San welcome the shamans' personal revelations of the spirit world even though they may be idiosyncratic; so, too, the ancient shaman-artists sometimes expressed unique insights in the form of depictions that are well out of the ordinary.

One of the most striking of these idiosyncratic paintings develops the idea of the eland as the principal symbol of the supernatural potency

shamans harnessed to enter the spirit world of trance. It shows four eland uniquely surrounded by zigzags. Because we know from neuro-psychological research that shamans in trance see zigzag entoptic phenomena, and because we know from San ethnography that shamans say they are the only ones who 'see' supernatural potency, it seems likely that a particularly sensitive, or adventurous, shaman-artist not only interpreted his entoptic zigzags as supernatural potency emanating from hallucinatory eland, as many shamans may have done, but actually recorded his insight in this remarkable painting. The painting is in fact a typical Stage 3 hallucination (p. 57). But there is more to his vision. A female eland lies upside down, dying, bleeds from the nose, and apparently urinates as its life ebbs away and it loses control of its bladder. Numerous paintings of dying eland show blood falling from the nose, but this is the only known instance of a dying eland being depicted urinating. As Dowson and Anne Holliday point out in an article on this painting, the artist seems to have been extending the more usual

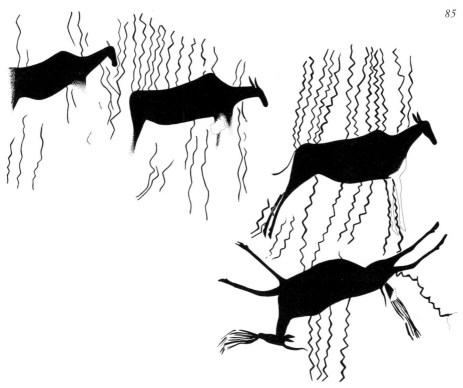

An Orange Free State rock painting of four eland surrounded by zigzags.

ways of depicting the idea that a dying eland releases its pent-up potency and that shamans can use this potency for a particularly powerful trance experience. Ordinary San people who saw this painting obtained from it a new understanding of supernatural potency.

Research of this kind will contribute to a more nuanced account of San rock art. A great deal of recent research has shown that the fundamental ideas underlying San rock art derive from trance experience, concepts of power, different ways of depicting the spirit world and so forth. This general work, an essential preliminary, has revealed the framework for much of the art. But any blanket, overall statement will obviously conceal the variations and subtleties, many of them personal, in the art. We must therefore move on to discern and explain the differences between regions, between techniques such as painting and engraving, and, then, within these broad categories, between individual depictions.

Once we accept that the art cannot be separated from real, individual people with their own insights into religious experience, we have to ask about the fate of those people. Towards the end of the eighteenth century, Sir John Barrow was struck by the gulf that seemed to exist between the beautiful rock art and the starving, impoverished San who remained. A San man questioned in 1821 by a deputy landdrost explained that there was no alternative to stealing stock from the invaders because they had no other means of subsistence. The white colonists had shot out the game, and their herds and flocks had destroyed the veld foods. Barrow said that the sufferings of the San at this time 'from cold and want of food were indescribable … they frequently beheld their wives and children perishing with hunger, without being able to give them any relief'.

Dia!kwain, one of Lucy Lloyd's San teachers, gave her a poignant personal account of this period. An accomplished shaman rain-maker, !Nuin-/kuiten, who had taught Dia!kwain's father how to make rain, met his end through his implicit belief in traditional San religion. Genuinely believing himself to have turned into a lion, he had killed a farmer's ox. The farmer raised a commando, and !Nuin-/kuiten was mortally wounded. Nevertheless, he managed to make his way back to his camp, and, as he lay dying, he begged Dia!kwain's father to keep up the rain-making tradition and to continue singing the power songs he had taught him. It appears that !Nuin-/kuiten made rain by singing these songs and playing a musical bow, as did /Kaunu (pp. 30–1), because the first part of his name means 'bow string'. It is common for San people to have such nicknames. After !Nuin-/kuiten's death, Dia!kwain's father used to say that he no longer felt the string vibrating in him as it did when !Nuin-/kuiten 'had called forth the rain-bull'. This is how Dia!kwain's father expressed his grief:

People were those,
Who broke for me the string.
The place does not feel to me,
   As the place used to feel to me,
   On account of it.

   For,
The place feels as if it stood open
   before me,
Because the string has broken for me.
Therefore,
The place does not feel pleasant to me,
   On account of it.

The commando that killed !Nuin-/kuiten was one of the last. Towards the end of the eighteenth century the farmers had started mounting terrible punitive commandos, killing the San as if they were vermin. Despite historical evidence to the contrary, some books on rock art still keep alive the opinion that the San were 'inveterate cattle thieves' who were incapable of

A   **B**

Newcomers appear in San rock art. A: A black farmer carrying a shield (eastern Cape). B: A man on horseback (Natal Drakensberg).

respecting other people's property. Overlooking the fact that it was San land in the first place, one rock art writer recently went so far as to say, 'The [San], who were the aggressors in most cases, … lost out in the end.' In his view, their fate was tragic but their own fault. Contradicting this misunderstanding, a government report dated 1835 states that attempts at conciliation would have succeeded, but 'The colonists were generally averse to pacific measures [because] the Bosjesmen they carried away, by means of the commandos, [had] numbers of children whom they were used to keep as servants.' The

destruction of a society to provide cheap labour has been a recurring theme in southern African history.

How did the shaman-artists of this troubled time respond to the incursions being made into their territory, the extermination of their game and the carrying off of their children? For centuries they had entered the spirit world of trance to fight off threatening shamans and evil spirits who sought to shoot mystical, invisible arrows of sickness into people. These spiritual conflicts are painted in the rock shelters. Some-times they depict two groups of bowmen, often with one or more of the clues that tell us this is not simply a narrative painting of a 'real' fight. In other cases they show men fighting off shamans in the form of lions, but again often with some pointers to the spirit world. When the colonists came on the scene, horses, rifles, wagons and other new items began to appear in conflict paintings.

For many years these contact period paintings were seen as strong evidence for the narrative approach to the art: they were taken to be straightforward records of traumatic experiences. There are good reasons for doubting this explanation. One hundred and fifty years ago, the missionaries Arbousset and Daumas noted that the San performed the trance dance or 'dance of blood', as they called it, 'before going to war'. At one time this statement was thought to be a misunderstanding based on popular Western notions of 'primitive' people performing war dances, but close examination of the art has since suggested that the two missionaries were correct. Colin Campbell has shown that, even if some paintings were closely connected with historical events, there are often, as in the more traditional paintings of fights between groups of bowmen, elements that suggest the shamans were still playing some role. As for centuries they had used their power to fight off

Newcomers in San rock art. A: A man shooting at fleeing San (Natal Drakensberg). B: A wagon drawn by a team of horses (western Cape).

threatening spirit shamans and lions, they now used the same powers to repulse the invading colonists. Depictions of trance experiences in which they engaged the newcomers therefore included horses, rifles and so forth.

The same pattern is being repeated in parts of the Kalahari today. Mathias Guenther has heard trancing shamans shouting out the vehicle registration numbers of white farmers whom they dislike. They are using their traditional powers to protect themselves from new threats in the same way that the shaman-artists of the nineteenth century used their skills to protect themselves from invaders.

But the rifles and horses in the shaman-artists' paintings were real enough and, in the end, the commandos were successful. Although many were absorbed into the white, black and so-called coloured populations, the southern San were virtually exterminated. To the north, where some other groups still survive in the less hospitable Kalahari Desert in Namibia and Botswana, matters are not much better. Although active extermination declined after World War One, farmers continued to capture San and to make them work on their farms into the 1950s. In Namibia the Ju/wa San lost most of their land in 1970 when the South African administration established, as part of its apartheid policy, a San 'homeland' that is just over half of their traditional land. The population density soared from one person in 37.5 square kilometres to five people in 1 square kilometre. The western two-thirds of this area has no surface water; the uncertain watertable lies between 300 and 1 000 metres below the surface. Hunting and gathering as well as farming are impossible.

In 1978 the South African Defence Force established a military base in the area, and many San people felt they had no option but to join the army and be drawn, much against their will, into the conflict. The army exploited their legendary tracking skills and encouraged them to think of the

San people at Tshum!kwe, Namibia (Photograph: Claire Ritchie, Ju/wa Bushman Development Foundation).

Huts built for the San at Tshum!kwe, Namibia in the 1980s (Photograph: Claire Ritchie, Ju/wa Bushman Development Foundation).

South West African People's Organization (SWAPO) as 'the enemy'. High army wages soon led to inequality, jealousy, drunkenness and violence. The dilemma brought by South African militarisation is expressed by ≠Toma in John Marshall's film *N!ai*, the life story of a !Kung woman:

The soldiers will bring fighting here. We're good people. We'd share the pot with SWAPO. But these soldiers are the owners of fighting. They fight even when they play, and I fear them. I won't let my children be soldiers, the experts at anger.

Most of the people in the area set aside for the San have not hunted or gathered for three or four generations. It is popular books and films that keep alive the myth that the Kalahari is still an idyllic land of people living close to nature. The media portray them wearing skins and clutching bows and arrows, unable to comprehend the modern world, baffled by Coca-Cola bottles. They are never shown as dispossessed and suffering grinding poverty, yet, at the same time, struggling to establish themselves as farmers.

When the Marshall family went to the Kalahari in 1950, there were about a thousand San people living a traditional hunting life: today there are none. To assist the San to build up herds and establish themselves in a vastly changed world, the Marshalls and others established the Ju/wa Bushman Development Foundation. Although the Foundation has had considerable success, much remains to be done. The false but widely held belief that the San are incapable of making the transition to farming is a major stumbling-block to development projects. Many people still regard the San as inherently naive, simple and superstitious people whose understanding of the world will never change. A San man expressed the problem like this: 'It is time for us to speak for ourselves and for you to listen to us. To understand each other, people should sit together and talk and then they should talk again.' Now, with Namibian independence a reality, the time for talking rather than fighting has at last come, and the San are beginning to take their place in the new social order. No one knows what their future will be.

Dominating races have to find a way to justify the subjugation and exploitation of others. In southern Africa, colonial thought presents black people as a faceless mass; the only individuals who appear in school textbooks are 'tyrants'. In this way the enormous suffering of millions of individual men, women and children is obscured. The San are treated differently: they are presented as inarticulate children. Thomas Pringle, for instance, in a poem admired by Coleridge, wrote about how he loved to ride through the desert with a 'silent Bush-boy' at his side. Nor is this failure to see San people as fully adult and responsible a thing of the past. In a recent and widely disseminated collection of San 'tales', the writer tells 'parents and teachers' that the stories are like rock paintings: 'Children sense in them a kinship for which there is no rational explanation.' Absurdly, the stories are said to be 'simple, totally free from abstraction – truly primitive art'. Complex San religion is brought down to the level of bed-time stories for Western children.

It is a great tragedy that so many books on southern African rock art encourage this racist view. As one author put it: '*It is perhaps natural to*

expect that Bushman art and child art should be much the same' (emphasis added). To be fair, he did go on to emphasise some differences between San art and child art. Writers who present the rock art as the work of idle, childish hands chronicling the trivia of primitive life underwrite, no doubt unwittingly, the belief that the San have not yet 'grown up' and therefore have few rights. Paintings and engravings are reduced, as some writers have put it, to 'singularly beautiful home decorating' or the product of an artist's simple, childlike desire to 'see again … what pleased him at first view'. In this book I have tried to show that this is indeed very far from the truth. San rock art is no less complex than, say, Italian quattrocento art. Its symbolism is as subtle, its concepts are as profound, its aesthetics as striking.

The lesson to be learned from a study of San rock art is this: the San's intellectual and aesthetic achievement on the rocks of southern Africa is second to none and clearly gives the lie to many myths about them. That was certainly the opinion of Wilhelm Bleek who knew the nineteenth-century San so well. Having read Orpen's account of his interviews with Qing, Bleek, unlike the writers of many modern books, recognised that San rock art was not, as he put it, 'the mere daubing of figures for idle pastime'. On the contrary, it had a 'higher character' and was part of San religion.

Today, 110 years later, the string that vibrated across southern Africa, calling up life-giving rain, is irreparably broken, and the few remaining San of the Kalahari are at the end of their tether. Although some still cling to their main religious ritual, the trance dance, it will not save their traditional way of life. As one woman put it, 'Death is dancing with me.'

Kalahari San in the 1950s (Photograph: Lorna Marshall).

11

Fragile heritage

The traditional San hunting and gathering way of life is now a thing of the past. All that remains is their rock art, scattered through the rock shelters and over the hilltops of southern Africa. This art is one of our most precious heritages. It is also among the most fragile.

What we see today is only a remnant of the glory that once illuminated southern Africa. Occasionally we come across an exceptionally well-preserved panel that gives us some glimpse of that past glory. One such panel is preserved in the South African Museum, Cape Town. It was removed in 1918 from the farm Linton in the north-eastern Cape. This was no easy task. As Mr G. S. T. Mandy, the person commissioned by Dr Louis Peringuey, Director of the Museum, to remove the paintings, wrote, 'They had to be carved out of the solid rock and in most awkward positions.'

Today very little remains in the Linton rock shelter. To remove the 2,00 x 0,75 metre slab, 1,5 metre of rock had to be destroyed on either side. Painted remnants beyond the destroyed area suggest that the parts

chiselled away were as richly painted as the preserved portion. Although we may lament the loss of these paintings, the extremely poor preservation of remnants elsewhere in the shelter shows that, had the slab not been removed, next to nothing of what is almost certainly the greatest rock art panel in any museum anywhere in the world would remain. Mr Mandy told Dr Peringuey that the cost of removal would be about £30, but that 'the painting will be worth any money if successfully removed'.

He was right. But this and some other well-preserved panels testify eloquently to the extent of the destruction of southern African rock art. Both paintings and engravings are disappearing at an alarming rate through natural weathering as well as through thoughtless human activities.

Ultimately, there is nothing that can be done to stop natural weathering. The geomorphological processes that formed the caves in the first place cannot be arrested: eventually all the paintings will be destroyed as the caves erode back into the hillsides. Unless panels are removed, as was the Linton slab, little will remain by, say, the middle of the next century. At the moment there is neither the interest nor the money nor the institution to mount such large-scale rescue operations. But some more immediate short-term measures are possible.

Research conducted by the National Building Research Institute of the CSIR showed that water is the principal destroyer of paintings. A few centimetres behind the walls of caves the rock is saturated. This water contains a high concentration of minerals and salts, and, as it soaks out and evaporates, it deposits these substances on the paintings. At the same time, the water dissolves the minerals cementing the tiny grains of sand that make up the sandstone on which so many of the paintings have been executed. The grains fall away and the paintings become fainter and fainter. Because some of the paints the San used soaked into the rock, this process can continue for a while without much noticeable effect on the paintings, but, when the critical depth is reached, the paintings disappear rapidly. This is why painted panels fade differentially, some paintings disappearing while others remain apparently unchanged: it all depends on the paint and how far it soaked into the rock. White and black paint are the most fugitive because they do not seem to have penetrated as deeply as the red. When one looks at a red monochrome eland, for instance, one must remember that it may well have had black hoofs, horns and a line along its back. Sometimes the black and white paint of polychrome eland disappear completely, leaving only the red body. Often the surface of painted panels appears to have flaked off. Whilst it is true that flakes, or spalls, do sometimes fall off the rock face, many of the 'flaked' areas actually increase in size quite gradually. It is factors like these that make nonsense of long-term projects to 'monitor' the fading of paintings in order to calculate how long they will last. 'Monitoring' fading rock art is no more than standing by and watching the inexorable progress of processes we already understand.

Often very well-preserved panels have survived because the bedding and joint planes of the rock behind the face have drained away the moisture in the rock before it could reach the surface. Where water actually runs down the face of the rock and over paintings, destruction is at its greatest. To prevent this process, the National Building Research Institute installed ridges, or gutters, on the ceilings of some caves to divert the flow of the water. But it is, of course, recognised that this is not a permanent answer to the problem.

If nothing can be done to arrest the natural processes of weathering that will eventually destroy all the

Orange Free State rock paintings damaged by vandals (Photograph: **P. den Hoed**).

paintings, something, one feels, can surely be done to prevent the much more immediate destruction being caused by people. Visitors to the painted caves often scratch their names across the art, touch and even lean up against the paintings, and blacken the walls with smoke from their camp fires. Farmers sometimes use painted caves as kraals; it is not long before the sheep and cattle destroy the paintings by rubbing against them. Principally at rock engraving sites but also at painted sites, people try to remove pieces of the art so that they can keep them as souvenirs. All too often they merely destroy the art. But the wetting of paintings in an attempt to make them clearer is perhaps the major factor contributing to their destruction. Rock art researchers themselves have not always been guiltless, despite their awareness of the disastrous effects of this practice. Walter Battiss was filled with horror when he saw for himself just how destructive water can be. In April 1944 he wrote to Professor van

Riet Lowe:

My heart has been sick over something that happened. When I wet with the Abbé's sponge a white painting of a zebra to see it more clearly, THE WHOLE ANIMAL WASHED AWAY!! And the black nearly went too. So now I am dreadfully afraid to wet anything anymore in case I destroy something and am accounted a vandal.

Battiss learned his lesson, but nearly half a century later the practice continues unabated and with cumulative effect. Perhaps people do not realise that all rock art is protected by law: heavy fines or imprisonment await those caught damaging sites. All cases of vandalism should be reported to the police as soon as they are discovered.

Why do the people of southern Africa seem to have so little respect for San rock art? As we have seen, right from the beginning of the colonial period the San were considered to be no more than children, perhaps even closer to the animals than to humankind. Consequently, their art has been seen as nothing more than the idle daubing of 'primitive' people. Against this background, it is small wonder that no value is attached to the paintings and engravings. For many people some paintings and engravings may be beautiful, some may be amusing, but most are unintelligible and worthless.

If people could come to appreciate the art as a religious expression of

Northern Cape rock engravings damaged by vandals (Photograph: T. A. Dowson).

Factories encroach on a rock engraving site at Vryburg (Photograph: T. A. Dowson).

great subtlety and genius, it is possible that the tide of vandalism could be turned and that at least some panels could be saved so that people at the end of the next century will be able to marvel as we do. To achieve such a profound change in values will not be easy. Western, highly industrialised nations do not consider people with less developed technologies of much account, even though their achievement in other fields may equal or even surpass those of the West. For one thing, different emphases are needed in school textbooks, emphases that will alert pupils to our common humanity with the San and encourage a respect for a religion that may seem to be very different from the so-called 'higher religions'. San rock art may

not be *your* heritage in the sense that it was made by your direct ancestors or even that it comes from a broadly similar cultural background, but we can all nevertheless come to understand and respect it as in no way inferior to our own traditions. In the last analysis, it was made by people very like ourselves.

The rock art of southern Africa should be seen and preserved as a sacred memorial to a lost people. But perhaps not only to the San, for they represent all whose way of life was destroyed by Western expansion. Their art may delight and intrigue, but it also admonishes. Even the most faded paintings and engravings, barely visible on the rock, are a clear call to eradicate the prejudice, selfishness and cruelty that still flourish in southern Africa. This fragile, fading heritage, so often misunderstood, so often trivialised, has something to say to all of us, irrespective of our social status or cultural background.

This book ends on a sombre note. The previous chapter was a farewell to the San people's traditional way of life. This one is – almost – a farewell to their art: we are discovering San rock art too late.

Suggested reading

There are many well-illustrated books on southern African rock art. The following have been selected because they include up-to-date research.

Dowson, T. A. In press. *Major Rock Engravings of Southern Africa.* Johannesburg and Cape Town: University of the Witwatersrand Press and David Philip.

Fock, G. J. 1979. *Felsbilder in Südafrika (Teil I).* Köln: Bohlau Verlagsanstalt.

Fock, G. J., and D. Fock. 1984. *Felsbilder in Südafrika (Teil II).* Köln: Bohlau Verlagsanstalt.

Fock, G. J. and D. Fock. 1989. *Felsbilder in Südafrika (Teil; III).* Köln: Bohlau Verlagsanstalt.

Garlake, P. S. 1987. *The Painted Caves: An Introduction to the Prehistoric Art of Zimbabwe.* Harare: Modus.

Johnson, T., and T. M. O'C. Maggs. 1979. *Major Rock Paintings of Southern Africa.* Cape Town: David Philip.

Lewis-Williams, J. D. 1983. *The Rock Art of Southern Africa.* Cambridge: Cambridge University Press.

Lewis-Williams, J. D., and T. A. Dowson. 1989. *Images of Power: Understanding Bushman Rock Art.* Johannesburg: Southern Book Publishers.

Pager, H. 1971. *Ndedema.* Graz: Akademische Druck.

Pager, H. 1989. *The Rock Paintings of the Upper Brandberg, Part 1: Amis Gorge.* Köln: Heinrich Barth Institut.

Vinnicombe, P. 1976. *People of the Eland.* Pietermaritzburg: Natal University Press.

The following books are recommended for background information on the San:

Biesele, M., and P. Weinberg. 1990. *Shaken Roots.* Johannesburg: EDA.

Bleek, D. F. 1924. *The Mantis and His Friends.* Cape Town: Maskew Miller.

Bleek, W. H. I., and L. C. Lloyd. 1911. *Specimens of Bushman Folklore.* London: George Allen. (Reprinted by C. Struik, 1968)

Guenther, M. 1986. *The Nharo Bushmen of Botswana: Tradition and Change.* Hamburg: Helmut Buske Verlag.

Katz, R. 1982. *Boiling Energy: Community Healing among the Kalahari Kung.* Cambridge, Mass.: Harvard University Press.

Lee, R. B. 1984. *The Dobe !Kung.* New York: Holt, Rinehart and Winston.

Lee, R. B., and I. De Vore. 1976. *Kalahari Hunter-Gatherers: Studies of the !Kung San and their Neighbors.* Cambridge, Mass.: Harvard University Press.

Marshall, L. 1976. *The !Kung of Nyae Nyae.* Cambridge, Mass.: Harvard University Press.

Marshall, J., and C. Ritchie. 1984. *Where are the Ju/wasi of Nyae Nyae?* Cape Town: Centre for African Studies, University of Cape Town.

Marshall Thomas, E. 1988. *The Harmless People.* Cape Town: David Philip.

Tobias, P. V. (editor). 1978. *The Bushmen.* Cape Town: Human and Rousseau.

Addresses

Readers interested in supporting the surviving San should contact the Ju/wa Bushman Development Foundation, 11 Divinity Avenue, Cambridge, Mass. 02138, United States of America. Or: P.O. Box 9026, Windhoek, Namibia.

Rock art discoveries should be reported to your nearest museum or to one of the following institutions:

Rock Art Research Unit, Department of Archaeology, University of the Witwatersrand, Johannesburg, 2050.

Department of Archaeology, University of Cape Town, Rondebosch, 7700.

Department of Archaeology, University of Stellenbosch, Stellenbosch, 7600.

As with all archaeological remains, rock art falls under the jurisdiction of the National Monuments Council, P.O. Box 4637, Cape Town, 8000.

The South African Archaeological Society (P.O. Box 15700, Vlaeberg, 8018), which has both amateur and professional members, exists to promote archaeology and disseminate archaeological information. The *South African Archaeological Bulletin* and the Society's newsletter, *The Digging Stick*, carry articles on rock art. In addition, the Society has local branches in the western Cape, southern Cape, Natal and the Transvaal, which organise regular lectures, outings and other archaeological activities.

Index